Simple Wooden Toymaking

Bob Mathias

HAMLYN

LONDON · NEW YORK · SYDNEY · TORONTO

To Helen and Philip, who exercised
incredible patience during the writing
of this book; never knowing where the
toys were destined to end up.

Published by
The Hamlyn Publishing Group Ltd,
London · New York · Sydney · Toronto
Astronaut House, Feltham, Middlesex, England.

© *Copyright The Hamlyn Publishing Group Limited 1974*

ISBN 0 600 34446 0

Printed in England by Chapel River Press (IPC Printers), Andover,
Hampshire

Contents

Introduction

The prime function of a toy should be to amuse a child and to stimulate the imaginations they all possess. Teaching toys play a valuable role in the education of children, but in my view the current emphasis on toys of this nature has been carried to the extreme.

This was one of the first thoughts I had when I was asked to write this book. As a result I have tried to create the sort of toys that can be enjoyed without there being an obligation to learn. Children remain children for too short a time for it all to be spent on the practical and useful. Let them waste some of it on the more unproductive activities; having fun and believing in the make-believe.

If you are interested in making things and can ally this to an interest in children, then start making toys and reap the rewards. If you are a novice, don't be put off by your lack of experience. If previous excursions into the craft of woodwork proved unsuccessful, re-assure yourself by looking at the creations of children. Their standards are not as fettered or influenced by convention as are ours. And their imagination tends to overlook deficiencies in style and craftsmanship.

Whatever toy you choose to make will doubly delight the child who receives it. Initially there is the pleasure of having something new to play with; and secondly, and perhaps a more important aspect from the child's point of view, is the fact that you have made it – specially for him or her.

All the tools you are likely to need are listed in the first chapter, but start off by using the tools you already have available. No power tools of any description are required to complete the projects featured.

I have attempted to make the toys as attractive as possible, while at the same time keeping their construction simple and strong. I hope that among them, you will find something of interest to build. Alternatively, may they give you the inspiration to create your own designs. If this end is achieved my small effort has been worthwhile.

BOB MATHIAS, MARCH 1974

Tools & Equipment

The proper use of handtools requires skill. Master craftsmen take years to acquire the skill they display so casually. However, it is amazing how tolerant the poor handtool is towards the well-intentioned, but ham-handed, amateur.

I am not advocating the misuse of tools by saying this; merely am I saying that if you happen to fall within this latter category and your end results are not usually worthy of exhibition in the British Museum, do not despair. Provided that you are using the tool correctly it will be only a matter of time before it becomes familiar with the manipulations of your hand and responds accordingly.

It is always a good thing to shop around for the best tool you can find, and this is not necessarily the most expensive. There is a great variety of tools on the market and it is as well to seek the advice of someone who knows the subject well before making your purchase. Most of the men who serve behind the counters of hardware stores know what they are talking about and asking a few questions should put you on the right track.

I think it is wise to buy only the tools you need for any one particular job. By doing this you are not involved in a large initial expense, nor do you end up with a great range of obscure tools that you will never use. By buying your tools as you need them your tool kit will steadily build up into a very useful and functional workshop. Remember that a good tool will last you for years and give good service, but only if it is well looked after and maintained.

I am not going to attempt to give you a detailed description of all the tools available for woodworking use. In this book we will be dealing with most of the basic tools and I shall concentrate only on these, and any other specific tools that may be needed for the completion of the projects features. All of them have been designed to be made without the use of any power tools.

HANDTOOLS

These fall roughly into the following groups. Those necessary for marking out timber: rules, tapes and squares; the tools for cutting timber: saws and chisels; the tools for shaping and finishing timber: planes, files and sandpaper blocks; and finally the tools for fixing timber together: screwdrivers, hammers, etc.

Marking out tools

A good *steel rule* is a wise investment and it should be marked in both inches and millimetres and be two feet in length. Being steel the markings cannot be easily obliterated through constant

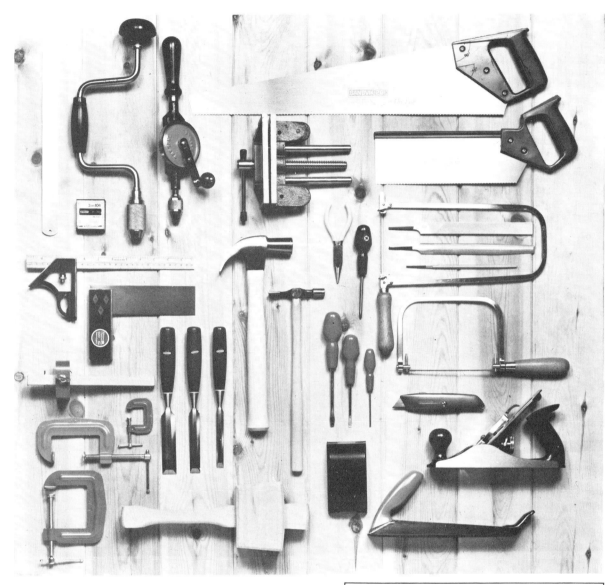

A selection of handtools

1. Steel rule
2. Flexible tape measure
3. Hand brace
4. Wheel brace
5. Combination square
6. Try square
7. Marking gauge
8. G-cramps
9. Bevel chisels
10. Wooden mallet
11. Claw hammer
12. Bench vice
13. Panel, or hand saw
14. Tenon saw
15. Fine-nose pliers
16. Pin hammer
17. Screwdrivers
18. Sandpaper block
19. Surform plane
20. Smoothing plane
21. Trimming knife
22. Coping saw
23. Fret saw
24. Files

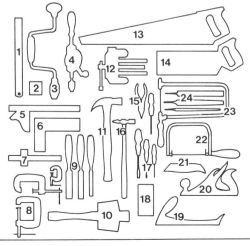

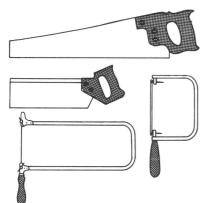

The three basic types of saw

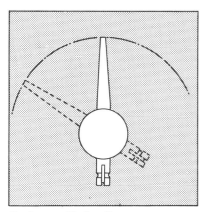

Coping saw blade adjustment

usage, and it will also serve as a true cutting edge when using a trimming knife on thin material, such as veneer or thin ply.

The try square is used for scribing right angles across your timber. Try squares can be either rigid or adjustable. I myself favour the adjustable square, sometimes referred to as a combination square, as these are more versatile and can be set to suit the width of material being marked, and also adjusted to a 45° angle.

A marking gauge is useful for scribing the positions of the cuts necessary for a joint, and also for marking lines parallel to the straight edge of a length of timber.

A flexible steel tape measure for measuring out your larger projects is more accurate than leap-frogging with the shorter steel rule. Also they are fun to play with when you are bored.

Cutting tools

The hand saw, or panel saw, is the largest of the three basic saw types you are likely to need. A cross-cut hand saw is suitable for all rough cutting jobs, both across and with the grain, and for general heavy-duty work. As a general rule the more teeth to the inch on a saw's cutting edge, the finer will be the cut. For a good general purpose hand saw choose one with ten teeth to the inch. Do not rush at the work when using a hand saw as this can lead to the saw wandering off course. Use a steady positive action, with an even pressure, and let the teeth of the saw do the work.

The tenon saw, as its name implies, is used for all fine cutting and jointing. It is a very rigid saw and has a strongly braced back to the blade. Blade lengths vary but a tenon with between 14 and 16 teeth to the inch is ideal for most purposes.

The coping saw is perhaps the most versatile saw of all. It will cut all manner of irregular shapes in a wide range of material thicknesses. The angle of the blade can be altered to suit the particular problem confronting you. The blades are disposable so no re-sharpening is ever needed; just replace the worn blade with a new one. The only disadvantage of the coping saw is that its depth of cut is limited by the distance between the blade and the frame.

The fret saw takes over where the coping saw leaves off. The very fine disposable blades are not nearly as strong as those used in the coping saw but it has a much greater range of cut and manoeuvrability. It is particularly suitable for cutting out enclosed areas of plywood, such as windows and doors. Should you contemplate making the doll's house, featured later in the book, then a fret saw will certainly be necessary for cutting out the smaller details.

These then are the saws you are likely to need. Treat them well and they will last you a lifetime. Whenever you have finished a job, and before you hang your saw back on its hook, give it a light coating of thin oil to protect it from the risk of rust; remember to wipe the saw clean before commencing work on your next project, otherwise you are likely to stain the timber.

Always keep a supply of spare blades in your workshop for the coping saw and fret saw. Nothing is more annoying than to have your last blade snap just before you have completed your last cut. This usually happens when all the shops are shut and you can't get a replacement.

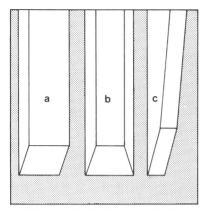

(a) Firmer chisel, (b) Bevel chisel, (c) Mortice chisel

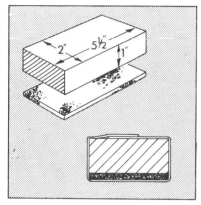

Making a simple sandpaper block

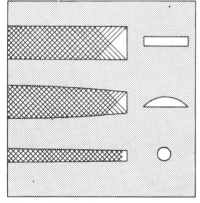

Three useful file shapes

Chisels. Many types and many shapes of chisel are available. But for our needs, and particularly if you are purchasing your first chisels, we need only concern ourselves with the bevel-edge chisel. This type will perform most jobs and is admirably suited for getting into tight corners. A range of sizes 1in., ½in. and ¼in. will prove the most useful.

Chisels should always be kept razor sharp as they quite quickly lose their cutting edge with use. A flat oilstone and a can of fine oil should be kept handy for re-sharpening.

Shaping tools

The plane is designed to give timber a smooth flat surface finish. The longer the plane the more likely it is that the surface is going to turn out true. A plane of about 10in. in length with a 2in. cutting edge is suitable for most smoothing jobs.

Sandpaper blocks can be purchased, but it is simplicity itself to make your own. All that is needed is a piece of softwood about 5½in. by 2in. by 1in. Very slightly chamfer the edges on one side only, and there is your sandpaper block. The chamfered edges avoid the risk of the block scoring the timber workpiece. The illustration shows an improved variation of this idea. Cut a piece of cork sheeting, about ⅛in. thick, to the size of your wooden block and glue it firmly with a contact adhesive to the block base. There will, of course, be no need to chamfer the base of the block in this case as the cork is not hard enough to damage your workpiece.

Having completed your block simply cut your sandpaper to the same length as the block. (A standard sheet will divide into four equal parts, each part being just the right size for the block.) It can now be tightly wrapped around the block and gripped firmly by the hand at each side.

A rasp or Surform tool is extremely useful for shaping curves and irregular shapes on timber. The problem with these two tools is that the results tend to be a bit on the rough side, and there is also the danger that your enthusiasm will carry you away and too large a cut will be taken.

I have used both of these tools but prefer to use a *flat file*. The cut taken is much finer and one does not need to spend so much time cleaning up the workpiece afterwards. The files I use, and would recommend, are a 10in. flat, a 10in. half-round and a ¼in. dia. 10in. round file.

Fixing tools

Screwdrivers come in a wide variety of shapes and sizes. A range of screwdrivers is always useful around the house, not only for woodworking. The important thing to remember when using a screwdriver is that the blade should always fit the slot in the screw being driven.

A Phillips or Posidriv screwdriver should also be part of your kit as these fit the increasingly popular cross-slot screws. Quite a few mechanical screwdrivers are available on the market, but they are not quite as easy to use as they seem to be. Their big disadvantage is their tendency to slip at the last moment and carve their way half-way through your beautifully finished timber.

A claw hammer is an essential in any toolkit; it should weigh about 16oz., the claw end being used for the extraction of bent

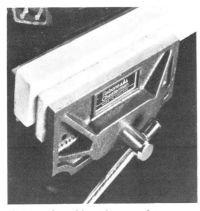

*Softwood packing pieces used to
protect a finished workpiece clamped
in a bench vice*

and unwanted nails. These hammers can be purchased with either
a steel or a wooden handle. Both types are admirable but the
wooden-handled hammer appears softer and seems not to impart
the same amount of shock to the wrist when used.

A pin hammer is needed for driving in very light panel pins.
It is very light itself and will not bend the pins nor damage the
work surface as would the larger, heavier claw hammer.

The hand drill or wheel brace is the last of the specific tools that
you are going to need. Once again you have a wide choice from
which to make your selection. Most hand drills are fitted with
a chuck designed to take a maximum $\frac{1}{4}$in. shank. A set of twist
bits, from $\frac{1}{4}$in. down to $\frac{1}{16}$in., and a rose bit for counter-sinking
screw holes, plus one or two larger wood bits with narrow shanks,
should fulfil all your drilling requirements. A later addition to
your tool kit could be a swing, or hand brace, which would
provide a much wider range of bit sizes.

Workshop equipment

A good work bench is a very useful item to have in your workshop.
However, you may not have either a work bench or a workshop;
I have neither. I do all my woodwork at the back of the garage
sandwiched between the car and an old chest of drawers which
serves admirably as my bench, it being of solid oak and weighing
about half a ton.

The primary requirement of any bench is that it should be
stable and not wobble about all over the place the minute you
touch it. You may not be as fortunate as I am in having an old
solid chest of drawers to work on, but any solid table or cabinet,
or a shelf strongly mounted to a wall, will serve the purpose.

The most important piece of equipment on your bench should
be a *bench vice*. This is going to be a tremendous aid to achieving
fine results. A good amateur woodworker's vice should be about
6in. long and should open between the jaws to a distance of at
least 4in. Make sure that your vice is bolted firmly to the bench.

Whenever you are gripping finished timber within the vice,
always ensure that it is sandwiched between two scraps of
softwood. This will avoid any chance of the finished timber being
damaged by the jaws; even plain jaws will mark the surface of
prepared timber.

To complete your workshop equipment all that you now need
are a couple of strong *G-cramps*. You can never have too many of
these but to start with we'll stick to just two. The smaller sizes
range from 2in. to 8in., this being the extent to which the jaws
will open. For our purposes two 4in. cramps will be sufficient.

TIMBER

Hardwood or softwood? Which one to use? I thought long and
hard about this question when I set out to write this book.
Hardwood is more expensive but more inclined to tolerate any
abuse dished out by the kids. Softwood is cheaper and easier
to work with but in some cases not quite as durable. Both types
have their advantages and disadvantages. I finally decided to
favour the softwood group for making the toys featured, and
perhaps the conclusions that led me to this decision will influence
you in yours.

Softwoods can be classified as those timbers cut from a cone-

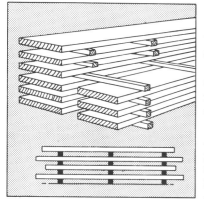
Scrap spacers between stored planks allowing a free flow of air

bearing tree, with needle leaf forms, a *coniferous* tree.

Hardwoods are those timbers cut from a broad leaf-bearing tree, *deciduous*. Although the above classification can be accepted as a general rule, as usual with general rules, there are exceptions. The Yew tree, classified as a softwood, is extremely hard and a lot harder than some actual hardwoods. Balsa wood, as you may know from your experience of model aeroplanes, is extremely soft, yet this tree is classified as a hardwood.

Economics played a large part in my decision to use softwoods. Although perhaps slightly less durable than hardwoods, one of the prime reasons for making toys yourself, apart from the fun of it, is to end up with a toy far cheaper than those sold in the shops. Softwoods are generally less expensive than hardwoods and, with the rapidly increasing prices of all timber types, this is not a factor to be ignored. Also, softwoods are more readily available from stock at timber yards and can be purchased in a wide range of ready-cut sizes. Some yards hold limited stocks of hardwood but more often than not one has to order this timber in advance.

When buying timber go to a yard in preference to a do-it-yourself shop as you will often find a marked difference in the prices charged. If you are buying softwood, or hardwood for that matter, don't order it over the 'phone as you may be disappointed with the quality of the delivered goods. Go to the yard and select the pieces you want from their stock. No good yard will object to this practice and it will establish you in their eyes as someone who is fussy about the quality of timber sought, and someone who cannot be foisted off with sub-standard goods.

Now that we have adopted the metric system a lot of cut timber is sized accordingly, and a table of equivalents appears on page 77.

Some yards now cut their timber to the nearest metre, so if you only want to buy 5ft. (approximately $1\frac{1}{2}$ metres), they will charge for the 2 metres from which this is cut. Find out whether your yard is one of these before making any purchase. If so, go elsewhere.

However, if you can afford it, always buy softwood to the nearest stock length, the excess won't be wasted. By adopting this procedure I have built up a comprehensive store of odd lengths and sizes from which I constantly draw for one job or another. Some of the scrap timber in my store is years old and really well seasoned and dry, and it never ceases to amaze me the uses to which it can be put.

Before using any timber it is essential that it has had ample opportunity to dry out thoroughly. Most yards store their timber in open-sided covered sheds. These are ideal for seasoning the timber but, in our climate, it does mean that newly purchased timber is sometimes a bit damp. With fresh planks it is best to store them flat with support spacers between them. This helps to avoid warping which sometimes happens if the planks are left free-standing.

Softwoods are much easier to work than hardwoods, but despite this advantage, one must remember to keep all cutting tools really sharp, as softwood tends to take the edge off planes and chisels very quickly. A good finish can be obtained on softwood and they will take a polish or stain well.

The final reason for my choosing to use softwood for the projects featured is that quite a lot of them have been given a paint finish and, to me, it seems a shame to cover the fine figuring on some hardwoods with paint, where a good softwood with indifferent figuring will serve as well.

The following table gives you a selection of the various timber types available and covers the ones you are most likely to need for the completion of all the toys featured.

TIMBER TYPE	CHARACTER	WORKABILITY	AVAILABILITY
(S) Douglas fir	gold/reddish brown, long and straight-grained, very durable	very easily worked provided all tools are kept sharp; is inclined to split	good
(S) Scots pine	pale yellow/red brown, straight-grained but can have many knots – needs selection	very easily worked, planes well over knots and does not easily split – is inclined to shrink if not properly seasoned	very good, common to most yards
(S) Spruce (whitewood)	cream/golden yellow, long, but occasionally erratic, grain – select carefully	easily worked but impossible when damp, takes all fixings well, does not easily split and finishes well	good
(S) Yellow pine (white pine)	pale yellow, smooth straight grain; few, if any, knots	very soft timber but easily worked – takes a very smooth finish – very stable	good
(S) Parana pine	cream/yellow/brown/ purple, straight-grained, occasional stream-bed knotting, very attractive figuring	fairly hard close grain but easily worked with sharp tools, takes a very fine polish, but in large sizes is inclined to distort; once distorted is impossible to correct	very good
(H) Oak (English)	light brown/brown, variable grain, long straight or knuckle	extremely hard and not really suitable for small work	to order
(H) Beech	white/light brown, close, straight, even grain	works very well, very popular with toymakers – durable and hard, inclined to split in the plank	to order at most yards
(H) Obeche	flaxen colouring, fairly soft, lightweight timber – straight-grained	easily worked but requires careful preparation before painting due to very open grain	fairly common
(H) Ramin	beige/off-white, close, very straight-grained timber	hard, but easily worked with sharp tools, very useful to the toymaker as it is sold in small stock sizes, stable but inclined to split, takes a high finish.	good

KEY: (S) Softwood, (H) Hardwood.

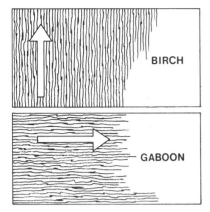

BIRCH

GABOON

Prefabricated boards

Added to the above are the various types of composition board; hardboard, blockboard, veneered boards and chipboards. A very useful and important type of composition board that we will be using is the old faithful, plywood. Most of the plywood produced today meets a British Standard specification and is generally very stable, although some of the thicker boards have a very slight tendency to twist from corner to corner. Plywood is still available in the non-metric 8ft. by 4ft. sheet, or cut to size from within this sheet.

Plywood can be purchased with surface veneers in oak, teak, sapele, mahogany and many others, but the two most common types we are likely to come across are gaboon ply and birch ply. The main difference between the two is that the gaboon, a mahogany-faced ply, will have the grain running down the longest dimension, whereas the birch ply has its grain running across the shortest dimension. This is useful to know before embarking on a large project where your grain direction is critical and the marking out of your ply sheet can only be done one way. Plywood should always be worked with care and should be cut with a fairly fine-toothed saw, such as a tenon, to avoid splitting too many of the fibres from the reverse side of the cut.

The above information should be regarded only as a guide to the various characteristics of timber types and it will be only by frequently handling timber yourself that experience will be gained.

ADHESIVES

Many people do not trust a glued joint. To them the answer to any fixing problem is a six-inch nail. In years gone by there was perhaps some justification for this attitude as some of the glue concoctions then prepared were, to say the least, a little suspect. Nowadays, however, there is no need to be distrustful of the many provenly successful brand names on the market.

Our main concern will be with the glueing of wood to wood, with a few exceptions, but it would be as well to bear the following points in mind before tackling any glueing process.

Always use the adhesive designed for the job. It is no use trying to glue furniture together with a polystyrene adhesive, nor is it very practical to mend broken china with balsa cement.

Having selected the right glue for your particular job, make a point of reading the manufacturer's instructions carefully. With a 'mix' glue, such as Araldite, this can be critical to the success of the operation.

Any timber to be glued must be clean, and free from all foreign matter such as dirt, grease, old paint and varnish, and most important of all, it must be dry. When repairing a broken joint it is necessary to remove all traces of old glue from the parts being worked on before applying the new glue.

With new work prepare the joints carefully; they should be close-fitting and nice and snug. The surfaces that are going to receive the adhesive should not have a high finish as this will lessen the chance of the adhesive biting into the grain of the wood; roughen over smooth areas before applying your glue to both surfaces.

Most of the projects dealt with in this book will not require clamping during glueing operations, but as a general rule it is wise to clamp a glued joint to maintain its correct setting. Do not clamp any joint too tightly or the adhesive will be squeezed out, resulting in loss of strength.

Finally, try to avoid over-glueing. It is not necessarily true to say that the more glue used the stronger will be the joint. Excess glue should be wiped off while still wet and kept away from the finished surfaces of your work. This is particularly important when working on an object that is going to be polished, as any excess glue remaining on the finished surface will act as a sealing agent and that part of the surface will not respond to the polish when applied.

I have listed below a selection of the adhesives you are likely to find most useful. They are listed under their brand names with brief details of their respective properties. If you have all of these in your workshop then there will not be many jobs around the house that cannot be tackled. These adhesives are relatively inexpensive and if stored in a cool, damp-free environment have an indefinite shelf life.

Araldite Twin Pack (Epoxy)

This is one of the strongest adhesives on the market and will stick virtually anything to anything. The Twin Pack consists of two tubes: one of resin and one of hardener which are mixed in equal parts. The resulting chemical reaction creates an immensely strong, waterproof, durable bond. The setting time is about 48 hours, but the reaction can be speeded up by applied heat (i.e. place the item being glued near a radiator). Excess glue can be wiped off with methylated spirits. I don't recommend the use of Araldite on large projects as this can be a bit expensive.

Cascamite

This adhesive comes in powdered form with the resin and the hardener already mixed. The glue is created by the addition of cold water. Read the instructions carefully before mixing as the amount of water used is critical. The resulting glue is very strong and waterproof, and is widely used in the boatbuilding industry. Apply the adhesive to both surfaces and allow a setting time of about 8 hours before disturbing. This glue is very suitable for large projects and has excellent filling qualities for those not-quite-perfect joints. Remove excess glue with hot soapy water before it dries.

Evo-stik Resin W

A very useful adhesive to have in your store, and the one I used on most of the projects featured in this book. It is quick setting, about 20 minutes, and completely dry within 24 hours. It is retailed in a handy plastic dispenser equipped with a spout that permits the application of just the right amount of glue. Although the bond is strong the glue is not waterproof so is not suitable for model boats or bath toys. Any excess can be wiped off with a damp cloth.

Balsa Cement

An old faithful with model makers but useful to have around when making toys. It is ideal for those small jobs like fixing the hair on tiny figures. Very quick-drying it is not suitable for anything requiring a really strong bond, nor is it waterproof.

Evo-stik Impact

As the name implies this adhesive sticks on impact, and once stuck is very difficult to shift, so make sure you position your two

components correctly first time. The adhesive should be applied
to both surfaces and allowed to become tacky before sticking;
this usually takes about 5 minutes. Most commonly used for
applying laminates to furnishings and not really suitable for a
wood to wood bond. Excess can be removed with acetone, or
your wife's nail varnish remover.

Polystyrene Cement

This is a special-purpose cement designed for use on rigid
polystyrene, and it is widely used for the very popular plastic
models on the market. It is, however, useful to have in one's
store, particularly when improvising with various materials to
create an attractive toy.

Working Methods

UNDERSTANDING DRAWINGS

One of the problems that confronts any designer, whether he be engaged on the design of a power station or a button, is the accurate representation of his design. The conversion, in other words, of the three-dimensional object he sees in his mind's eye into the two-dimensional drawing, or plan, from which this same object can be easily manufactured.

The reading of complex working drawings is, without doubt, a matter of some practice. This is usually coupled with a degree of knowledge of the subject matter featured on the drawing. With regard to the toys featured within this book, both the subject matter, and the drawings have, wherever possible, been kept in their simplest form. Each item is accompanied by a photograph and although this can never show the toy from all angles it will afford an extra point of reference. The types of drawing used throughout the book can be broken down as follows, and, if you are not too familiar with the mechanics of working drawings the following points will prove useful to you.

Straightforward sketches which I hope will show clearly the shape or function of an item, or a particular procedure being executed: some exploded views giving the physical break-down of an assembly: sections showing the construction of an assembly, and finally detailed plans giving accurate dimensions.

With some of the toys it has been sufficient to show it in sketch form but with others, where the dimensions are critical, it has been necessary to draw plans.

Plans

Basically the function of a plan is to show all aspects of an object from each of the relevant viewpoints. For example, a simple box with the corners cut off could only be manufactured if dimensioned views were drawn of the various faces affecting its shape. The principal view of any item is the view showing the base layout as seen from above. This is always referred to as the 'Plan View'. The views of the front and back and of the two sides are referred to as elevations, and are always labelled as such, i.e. 'Front Elevation'. Usually with a fairly simple object one is presented with just three views, the plan, the side elevation and the front elevation. Each of these will carry all the relevant information, dimensions, angles, etc., that are required to manufacture the item.

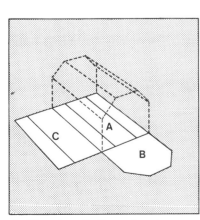

A. Plan view, B. Front elevation,
C. Side elevation

Sections

Suppose we now drill a hole half-way through our box. This

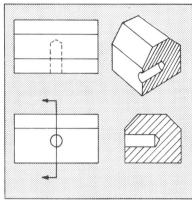

A sectioned view shown as an elevation and as a perspective

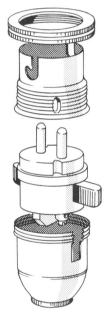

An exploded view

detail could be shown on any one of the views, but is very often given a sectional treatment on the view likely to supply the most information. A section is shown in the sketch both as a scale drawing and as a perspective view.

Exploded views
This type of drawing simply shows all the component parts of a composite structure, or assembly, but with each of these components exploded or pulled away from its location. An exploded view should also show each component in the correct order of assembly, and those featured in this book do so. The sketch shows this treatment given to a simple household light fitting.

Enlarging and reducing designs
It is impossible to give accurate dimensions when dealing with an irregular-shaped component, and in these cases it is necessary to adopt a different method of presentation.

Let us take for an example the simple animals on page 42. You will see that these irregular shapes have been drawn on a square grid background. Each of these squares, although reduced in size, represents a 1in. square. To enlarge one of these animals count the number of squares that its shape occupies, both vertically and horizontally, and number them as illustrated. Now draw out a fresh grid with the squares being drawn to full size and number these similarly; each of your squares should now measure 1in. It now remains for you to plot the design within your new grid by following the points where the animal's shape crosses each of the numbered lines. Finally join up each of your plotted points and you have successfully scaled up the animal's shape. The same procedure is adopted, only in reverse, for reducing the size of a design.

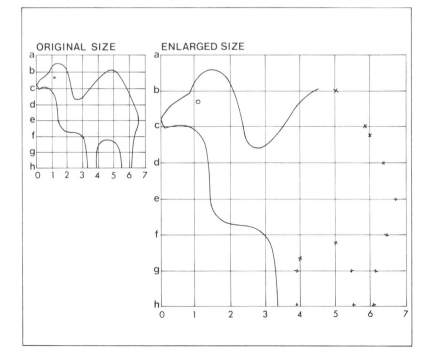

A grid system for enlarging and reducing an irregular shape

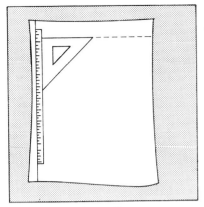

Establishing a datum line

MARKING OUT TIMBER

All marking out should be governed by a datum line and a brief description of this would be 'any fixed, accurate line from which all other dimensions can be drawn, and locations measured'.

On a large, new sheet of plywood or blockboard any one of the four, machine-cut, edges could be used as a datum line. But never take this for granted; check to see whether the edges are true with a steel rule. If all the edges prove to be out of true and not perfectly straight it will be necessary to draw a datum line.

Having established, one way or another, a true datum line to work from, your marking out can commence. Examine your timber carefully. Any flaws such as bad knots, splits and machine marks should be left in the waste (the excess timber areas not being used), and the sound areas of timber reserved for marking out your component part.

The try square is ideal for marking off lengths from small-section timber and if you have chosen to purchase an adjustable square its versatility will permit its use over a wide range of sizes. You will see from the sketch that it will also enable you to scribe a 45° angle, necessary when making mitre joints.

For actually marking your timber use either a scribing point or a soft pencil. Go easy with the point, especially if you're not scribing a cutting line, or you'll end up with a deep scratch. A soft pencil leaves a mark that is easier to see and also easier to sand off the finished surface.

For marking off certain joints, or for a strip of timber to be cut parallel to an edge, use a marking gauge. First set the gauge point at the correct distance (the width of the strip to be cut) from the block cheek and then tighten up the locking thumb-screw. With the cheek held tight up against the edge of your board run the gauge down the edge and so scribe your line. Without a gauge but with a little practice it is possible to execute the same procedure by using your finger as a guide along the cut edge of the timber.

Warning: Never forget the thickness of your saw when marking out. If you have four lengths of timber, 6in. long, to cut out; DON'T cut off a length 2ft. long and then divide it by four. This will result in a loss, somewhere along the length, of approximately $\frac{3}{16}$in. Cut each 6in. piece of timber separately.

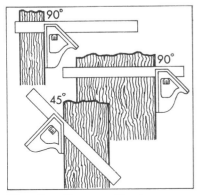

The adjustable, or combination, square

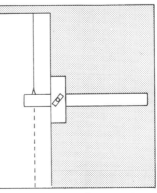

Using a marking gauge along an edge   *Avoiding accumulated error*

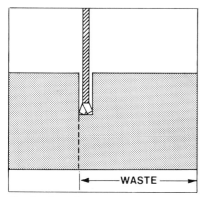
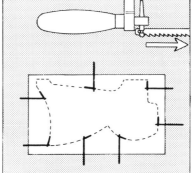
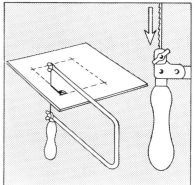

Cutting into the waste　　　*The versatile coping saw*　　　*Making an enclosed cut*

HINTS ON HANDTOOLS

We have already discussed the types of saw you are most likely
to need. They should be kept sharp at all times and always lightly
oiled with thin machine oil when not in use. It is best to hang
saws from hooks as this helps to keep their blades true and free
from unnecessary stress. Sharpening saws is quite a skilled job
so is best left to an expert. Most good tool shops provide this
service and it is relatively inexpensive. If it is necessary for you
to exert excess pressure in order to make your saw cut, then it
is time it was sharpened. A good sharp saw requires only a firm,
even pressure to execute a cut.

Never try to rush a saw along a cut or before long it will decide
to go its own way and wander off all over the place. If the saw
happens to wander on to the wrong side of your line it could
prove to be an expensive error. Always cut into the waste timber
and let the saw do the work.

On very long cuts, particularly when working with the grain,
your saw may tend to bind in its slot. If this happens, wedge
open the end of the slot to ease the pressure on the saw blade.
Don't overdo this wedging or the saw cut will rapidly turn into
a split.

When using the coping saw, the blade should be inserted to cut
on the push stroke, that is with the teeth facing away from you.
The sketch shows how the angle of the blade can be altered to
suit the cutting-out of an irregular shape. Whenever any
adjustment is made to the blade angle be sure to re-tighten the
screw handle completely before cutting and to make sure that the
two blade pegs are aligned. This ensures the blade cuts true.

The fret saw has a blade that is fine enough for you to cut
exactly to your scribed line. This saw is held in the horizontal
plane with the blade then being vertical. The actual cutting is
done on the downward or pull stroke, with the teeth facing
downwards. The sketch shows how to cut out an enclosed shape
using the fret saw.

Using a razor-sharp chisel can be very satisfying but it can
also be very dangerous so chisels should always be handled with
respect. Never leave them lying carelessly around with their
cutting edges unprotected – or within reach of children. With
most tools a child can come to little harm but the chisel is
definitely not for playing.

*Illustrated opposite : The Toytown
Soldiers with the Stunt Flyer and
the Car Ferry*

18

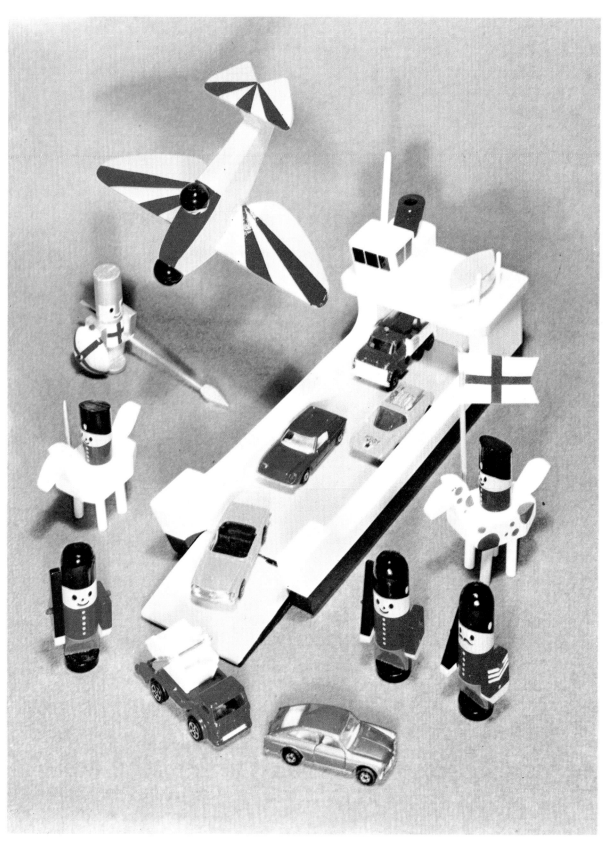

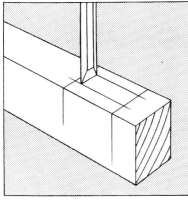

Cutting a mortise slot with a bevel chisel, the first cut a little way from the scribed line

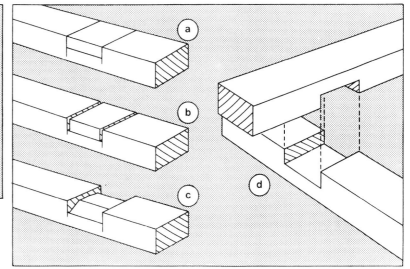

Above right : The four stages of cutting a half-housing joint, (a) the scribed joint, (b) saw cuts made to the marks, (c) the waste removed from both sides, (d) fitting the completed joint

Assuming we are using a bevel chisel to cut out a housing then the bevel should always face towards the waste. Position the chisel slightly away from your scribed line and a little into the waste, as you remove more wood from the housing work back towards your final line – a little at a time. Most of the chisels now sold are fitted with composition plastic handles and these will stand hammering from either a wooden mallet or a metal hammer. However, with a wooden-handled chisel it is advisable to strike it with a wooden mallet if you do not want to split the handle. On softwood, and with a sharp chisel, a moderate blow is all that is needed to make a positive cut – so don't smash away regardless. All joints should be tried for fit as you go. A too tight joint can always be eased a little but a sloppy joint is going to be with you for a long time, despite filling. The sketch shows the steps in cutting a half-housing joint which is used in the construction of the roundabout on page 68.

Housings that have been cut too tight can also be eased by using a flat file. Some flat files have teeth only along one of the edges so if you are using one of these, take care when working into a corner that the clean edge of the file is against the upright face of the corner; otherwise the file will undercut. A plank that has not had the end cut true can also be squared off with a flat file. Simply clamp the plank in the vice between two true pieces

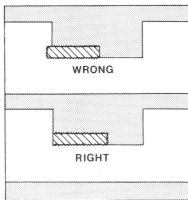

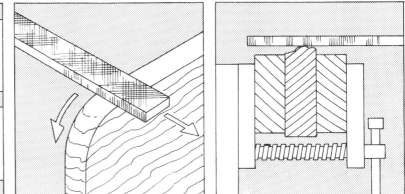

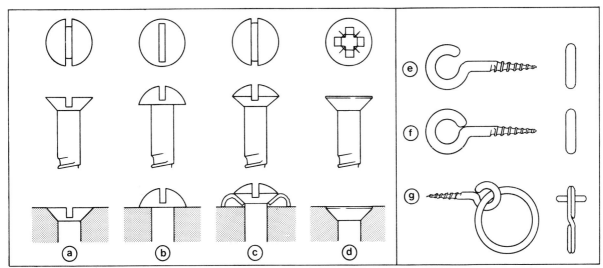

A selection of fixings : (a) a countersink or flathead screw, (b) a round-head screw, (c) a raised-head screw and screw cup, (d) a Posidriv screw, (e) a screw eye – open, (f) a screw eye – closed, (g) a screw ring

of scrapwood and file off the surplus. This practice can be adapted for planing a true edge on a plank but the scrap pieces will obviously then have to be the same length as the plank being planed.

Drilling

To drill a perfectly round hole is not very difficult if the following points are noted. If you have never used a hand drill before, practice a little on a piece of scrap.

Hold the hand drill firmly and apply only enough pressure for the bit to begin cutting. A sharp bit will do most of the work for you and will cut through your timber without much bother. Try to maintain a regular action whilst drilling, turning the wheel smoothly; try not to turn the wheel in a series of jerks and pulls. If you find that considerable pressure is needed to make your bit cut the timber, then it is probably blunt, and more likely to be tearing the timber than cutting it.

With a bit that is cutting well, ease off the pressure just as it starts to break through. By easing off you will allow the bit to cut away the final fibres and not risk splitting them by breaking through too fast. Try to maintain the drill at a constant angle throughout the drilling operation or the resulting hole will tend to be oval and not as round as it should be.

When drilling through very thin material it is very easy to split the fibres on the reverse side. To avoid this happening, clamp the thin workpiece to a solid piece of scrap and drill right through into the scrap.

It is sometimes necessary to drill a hole only part of the way through a piece of timber or to a specific depth. There is a very simple solution to this problem; simply wrap a piece of sticky tape around the drill bit at the required distance from the tip and start drilling. When the tape reaches the work surface the hole is at the correct depth.

A simple gauge for drilling a hole to a specified depth

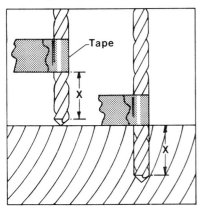

FIXINGS

Before fixing any two components together with screws, pilot holes should first be drilled. This is the procedure to follow. First select a drill bit of the same size as the shank of the screw

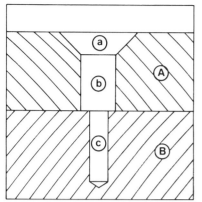

(a) Countersink, (b) Shank clearance hole, (c) thread pilot hole

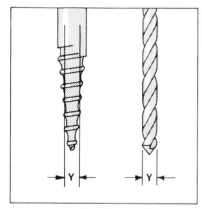

Assessing the size of a pilot bit

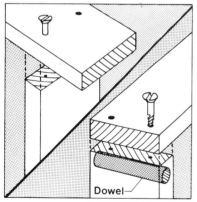

A simple butt joint and an improved stronger version of the same joint

Illustrated opposite : Two Simple Animals and a selection of simple figures

being used and drill right through timber piece A (see sketch). If you are using flat-head screws then this hole should now be counter-sunk with your rose bit. Next, drill a pilot hole in timber piece B to at least half the depth of the screw thread. This hole must obviously be smaller than the thread of the screw being used, and exact tables of sizes are available in more definitive works than this. However, as a general rule, aim to select a bit with a diameter roughly equivalent to the average diameter of the screw thread but excluding the teeth. The sketch shows how to assess this approximate size.

The base of the fort featured on page 59 is made with a series of butt joints. Each one of these butt joints necessitates a screw-fixing into the end grain of the timber. End grain does not give such a good bite on a screw as does a fixing into the side grain. Remember, therefore, to use a slightly longer screw with end grain to obtain the necessary strength. A pilot hole is seldom required when screwing into end grain unless you choose to use the refinement illustrated here, in which case it will be necessary. The dowel with its grain running across the width of the plank adds enormously to the strength of the joint.

Any screwdriver you use should always be the right size. That is, the blade should always fit the slot in the screw exactly. If the blade is too wide it will tear the wood surface as you drive the screw home, and if it is too small it may slip and damage not only the wood surface but also the slot in the screw. If the slot is damaged too much you may be left with a screw that can neither be driven in or out. With very small screws it is not necessary to drill pilot holes. A bradawl will serve to make a hole sufficient for the screw to bite. Alternatively a panel pin tapped in and then withdrawn will have the same result.

It is often extremely difficult to hold very small screws in position in order to drive them home successfully. A simple method of overcoming this problem is to push the screws through a strip of stiff grease-proof paper, with which you can hold the screw in position. Once the screw is secure the paper can be torn away.

Whether you choose to use steel or brass screws is largely a matter for you to decide, as far as our projects are concerned. I have generally specified steel screws throughout as they are considerably cheaper and a good deal stronger than brass. With exposed screws, brass is not quite so unsightly and can be used to good effect as a decorative feature. When using brass screws,

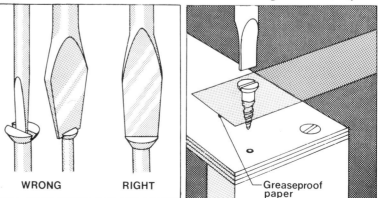

23

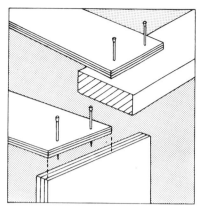

Pre-pinning thin plywood over scrap timber prior to final fixing

particularly on hardwood, first drive in a steel screw of the same size. This will pre-cut the hole for the brass screw and avoid excessive binding which, if your pilot hole is tight, could result in the brass screw snapping off. A spot of candle grease applied to a screw before driving also avoids binding. To remove old screws that look as though they may prove to be very stubborn, try giving them a further half-turn in, before attempting to screw them out. This is very successful and it often avoids the need for brute force.

Pinning

Panel pins by the nature of their function are usually very thin so don't smash them with a 2lb. hammer or you'll end up with a few dozen custom-made fish hooks. Hold the pin square on to the timber and tap lightly with a pin hammer until the pin has taken a bite into the surface of the wood. Then, holding the pin hammer at the foot of the handle and not just below the head, let the weight of the hammer tap the pin firmly home.

A pilot hole is sometimes advisable for a panel pin, particularly on thin mouldings. Many of these are now made from Ramin, which is quite a brittle timber and easily split, particularly if pinning close to a cut end. Brass pins also sometimes require a pilot hole, unless using very soft wood, as they tend to bend easily. If a pin is showing on the surface of your timber and you want it concealed, tap it lightly below the surface level with a centre punch or a stout wire nail with the point filed flat. When punching in pins on thin plywood take care not to go too far or the fixing will lose its strength and the pinhead will break through the plywood.

Pre-pinning

If you are pinning together two pieces of thin plywood, tap the pins right through your first piece of ply until they just break through the surface. This can be done on a piece of scrap timber. The slightly protruding points will now act as a useful guide when locating the two pieces together, as they can be pushed into position by hand, before being finally tapped home.

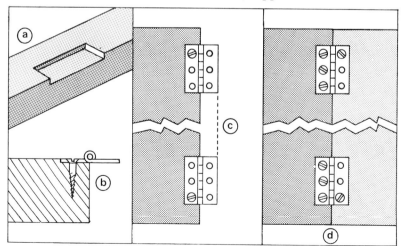

Fitting hinges : (a) hinge bedding slot, (b) correct position of hinge in slot, (c) initially aligning hinges, (d) final fixing

Improvisation

The ability to look at an object and to see it as potentially something entirely different is not an asset we all possess. It is, however, an asset that can be developed and refined. Sometimes it is carried to the extreme as is witnessed by the man who hit upon the notion of constructing a life-size model of the Forth Bridge out of old beer bottle tops. But with moderation we can all learn to develop the scroungers instinct and by a little judicial adaptation, here and there, use to good effect those items considered by others to be useless.

I am always on the lookout for things which might have a possible use, old broom handles, cardboard tubes, bits of string, wooden knitting needles, door handles, cocktail sticks, dowelling of all sizes, wooden balls, beads, bottle stoppers and a wealth of other bric-à-brac. Some of these items such as wooden balls and door handles are easily obtainable at do-it-yourself shops and I have put them to use on several of the projects featured in this book. Cocktail sticks are also cheap to buy and invaluable when it comes to the finishing of the smaller toys, which I talk about in the next chapter.

Cardboard tubes and broom handles can be transformed into steam engine barrels and castle turrets, and although a cardboard tube is not very durable their saving grace is that they are cheap enough to be expendable.

A selection of useful items

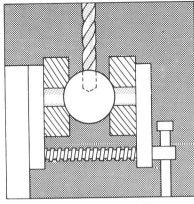

Drilling through a wooden ball, using softwood jigs made from scrap

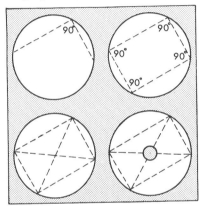

A simple method of finding the exact centre of a circle

Plastic wheel kit, axles and hub-caps. Made by Fobel Ltd.

Illustrated left: The Caveman Rocker, the Train Set and the Fairground Roundabout

Specific requirements

Certain projects lead one to look for specific things to solve a particular problem and this was the case when I was dealing with the doll's house (see page 63). Furniture is easy enough to put in but what about the little extras that make the doll's house more interesting and more fun to play with. I was pondering on the question of what to use for chinaware and I suddenly remembered seeing some small door handles in my local do-it-yourself shop. They were slightly dish-shaped with a small base underneath for screwing them into place. I purchased some of these and with the base cut off they made ideal plates and bowls. Their shape set me thinking and immediately one of them became a hat for the Chinaman on page 26 and a shield for the knight on page 19; I also found them to be quite successful as wheels for a pull-along toy.

Wheels

Having mentioned the subject of wheels it seems appropriate to discuss these in more detail. Plastic wheels can be purchased, and a very successful kit is marketed by Fobel Limited. This kit is comprised of the four wheels, the metal axle rod (cut to length, as required) and four chromium-plated hub-caps. The system covers a wide range of wheel sizes and the items can be bought separately or as a complete set. In most cases, I prefer to see a wooden toy fitted with wooden wheels, but, of course, there are exceptions.

It used to be possible to buy wooden wheels at most hardware shops and all model shops. This is not now the case and they are quite hard to come by, although some specialist wood-turning companies do still turn wheels to order. In my quest for the elusive wooden wheel I was forced to stretch my ingenuity to even greater lengths and devised the following methods and alternatives for making the various types of wheel featured on the following toys.

A wheel's prime requirement is that it should be round; it doesn't have to be flat. Here then was the first solution – wooden balls. These are readily available and come in a wide range of sizes from approximately 3in. diameter down to approximately $\frac{1}{2}$in. diameter. I say approximately as their dimensions are seldom exact. Care should be taken, when purchasing, to ensure that your potential set of wheels are all of the same diameter, as the wooden balls tend to vary very slightly in size – either larger or smaller than the stated dimension. They are usually of quite a good finish and need very light sanding before painting or otherwise finishing. As you will see from the simple figures on page 26, and the roundabout on page 23, their versatility does not stop at wheels.

Door handles we have already discussed, but another method of making wheels is to cut off thin slices of dowelling. If this is done with care, and the resulting disc rubbed across a piece of sandpaper to smooth it, the end product makes a very serviceable wheel. It is quite easy to find the centre with small wheels like these, but just in case you are a little inaccurate have a few spare slices of dowel ready cut. This method was used for the wheels on the flexible crocodile on page 54 and the train on page 26.

Cutting wheels from solid timber is another simple method

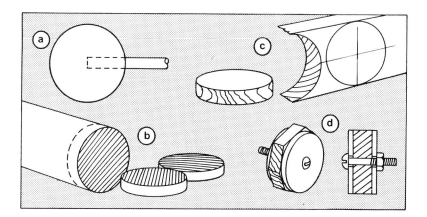

Improvised wheels: (a) ball wheel, (b) dowel wheel, (c) wheel cut from solid timber, (d) wheel shaped between two metal washers

provided the timber is first firmly clamped in your bench vice. Draw your circle to the diameter required. If you do not possess a compass to do this, draw round the base of a tin or bottle. Now cut as closely as you can all the way round the line. This can be done with either a coping saw or a fret saw depending on the thickness of timber being used. When the rough wheel is completely cut out, all that should be required is a general clean up all round with a flat file and finishing off with sandpaper. DON'T FORGET to mark your centres positively first. Smaller wheels can be made by sandwiching a piece of wood between two metal washers of an equal size. The centre hole facilitates the insertion of a fine bolt which clamps the assembly tightly together during the shaping process.

In desperation you can always use old wooden cotton reels and perhaps make yourself a toy steamroller (which is just about all you can make with an old cotton reel); but the holes through a cotton reel are seldom, if ever, centred accurately, and are of such a size as to make the axles very heavy looking.

Axles can be made from dowelling, this being free to revolve within the body of the toy and glued to each wheel, or alternatively glued within the body of the toy and the wheel left to revolve around the dowel. The latter method obviously requires a stop on each axle to prevent the wheel from dropping off. To avoid this, drill a small hole in the end of the axle and push in a small peg, make sure it is a good tight fit – this method is very successful. Wheels, such as those used on the train (see page 26), can be held in place with a small upholstery pin. This also looks quite smart and attractive. Finally, where it is essential for the wheel to turn smoothly but firmly, a screw can be used as an axle. Ideally, round-headed screws should be used with a small brass washer inserted either side of the wheel. The most important point to bear in mind is that the shank of the screw should be at least as long as the thickness of the wheel and slightly longer if possible. If the shank is too short and a part of the screw thread protrudes from the wood, within the wheel, it will have a tendency gradually to unscrew with use.

These, then, are just a few of the improvised methods I have found to be useful. As your toymaking experience grows, and your projects become more and more diverse, you will no doubt discover your own solutions to the various problems you are faced with.

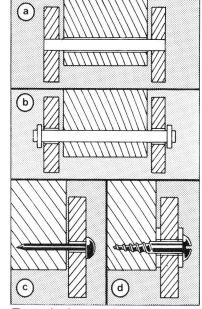

Types of axles: (a) fixed wheel on free axle, (b) free wheel on fixed axle, (c) upholstery pin axle, (d) screw axle

Finishing Techniques

Many a potentially fine-looking toy, perhaps involving many hours of painstaking effort, has been spoiled by a bad finish. The final effect of any toy can be ruined by the bad application of paint or insufficient preparation prior to painting. Nothing looks worse than paint applied to a toy that has been badly sanded down – the paint has no sparkle and the grain fibres stand up like a fur coat.

The decision as to what finish your toy is to have must be made fairly early on, as this is going to influence certain of the procedures you will have to undertake in its manufacture, and the order in which these procedures will occur. It is no use deciding on having a polished finish on a completely assembled toy unless the timber has previously been prepared for just such a finish. Further sanding done at this stage can only be partly successful; because of joints and awkward corners it will be virtually impossible to get a smooth run with your sandpaper, and the toy is bound to end up with a lot of cross-grain scratches. When the polish is applied to these scratches their appearance will be aggravated and not hidden.

Sanding

Always do your rubbing down in the same direction as the run of the grain, *never* across the grain. Use a softwood sandpaper block and preferably one with a cork base. Begin sanding with a coarse-grade paper and gradually work down to a finer grade, until the timber has the finish you require. If possible try to do the initial sanding before any cutting out is done. This will make the job easier as, the larger the piece of timber, the greater will be the possibility of getting a good run with your sandpaper block along the surface. Small component parts are much harder to sand down once they are cut out; hence this suggestion that the whole piece be sanded down beforehand. Obviously extra care will need to be taken with the pre-sanded timber to avoid marking the smooth surface. This is really a matter of common sense; use packing pieces in your vice and when marking out; make sure that the bench top has been cleared of any loose chips or bent nails, which could possibly cause damage.

A firm, even pressure should be applied and the sandpaper block moved along the timber in straight strokes, taking care to hold it flat all the time. The final sanding, prior to the application of a polish or a varnish, should be done with a very fine garnet or flour paper.

Making a toy that is going to have a natural finish, i.e. either polished or varnished, requires some thought about the order in

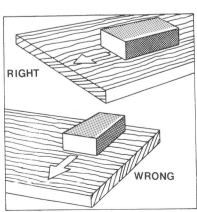

Sanding down with the grain

which it should be assembled. To avoid any problems occurring, during or after assembly, cut out all the parts from your pre-sanded timber and finish sanding them individually. They should be sanded carefully and particular attention should be paid to any sawn ends. Try to avoid rounding these off too much, which can easily happen. End grain, particularly on softwood, can be smoothed initially with a flat file before sanding. It is worth taking some trouble with end grain as usually it is very attractive and the figuring shows up well after polishing.

The sanding of very small components that are difficult to hold can be done in the following way. Lay a sheet of sandpaper on a flat, even surface, and then, holding the part firmly under your fingers, rub it across the sandpaper – making sure that the direction of the grain is the same as the direction you are rubbing. Take care to avoid applying an uneven pressure to any one side of the part or you will sand down too much from that side only.

Sanding a dowel rod can be done by holding a piece of sandpaper across the palm of the hand and then pushing the rod through the partly closed hand, turning the rod occasionally as you do so. Dowel rod is also very useful if you have need to sand out the inside of a drilled hole. Simply wrap the sandpaper round a piece of dowel, slightly smaller than the hole to be cleaned, and run it through; once again turning the dowel as you do so. Remember that freshly sanded wood should not be handled with greasy hands.

Filling

Where it is necessary to fill a particularly deep, open grain in order to achieve a smooth surface, it is worth purchasing a purpose-made grain filler. These fillers are ideal for use on a toy that is to have a natural finish – polish or otherwise – as they are either colourless or matched to specific timber types. If the toy is being painted, then there are alternative, more economical, methods available. Mix up a thin solution of varnish or oil-based undercoat with an equal amount of thinners and add to this a couple of spoonfuls of Polyfilla or fine-grade plaster. The resulting mix has a thick, creamy consistency and should be worked well into the grain. It is best applied with a piece of stiff card or a Formica offcut and spread over the entire surface. Surplus mix can be wiped off while still wet, leaving it remaining only in the grain. A very fine grain can be filled in the same way, using French chalk or talcum powder instead of plaster. This is not only effective, but also has the added attraction of making your project smell very nice!

For large holes and scars, or for filling in the holes left by sunken panel pins, use a wood-filler such as Brummer Stopping or Plastic Wood. Plastic Wood dries very quickly and once dry can be fashioned almost as well as the real thing, but allow for a very slight tendency to shrink if filling a large hole. In cases like this it is best applied in thin layers, each one being built up on the preceding one until the hole is filled, and allowing each layer to dry before applying the next. For filling very large gaps (which all of us have to contend with on occasions), an ideal mixture is an equal volume of adhesive, such as Cascamite, mixed with sawdust. It should be left to dry thoroughly before further working. Holes resulting from deeply countersunk screws are best plugged with a short length of dowel rod and cleaned up after the adhesive has completely set.

Polishing

We will be dealing with wax polish only and as a first application this should be applied liberally. It should be applied with a soft, lint-free cloth and worked well into the wood, particularly into the end grain. It should be left for about an hour to soak well in and then any surplus remaining on the surface wiped off and a second coat applied. This second coat can be buffed-up to a smooth finish and if required a third, and final coat, applied in the same manner. Teak oil will also give a very attractive finish to bare wood and is applied with either a loose cloth or a cloth pad.

Varnishing

As with polishing, the timber surface should be smooth, clean and totally grease-free. As an added precaution, and before applying your first coat of varnish, wipe over the timber with a cloth soaked in white spirit to remove any remaining dust particles and to make the surface fully receptive to the varnish.

The first coat should be thinned with an equal proportion of thinners and applied with a soft-haired brush. It should be worked well into the wood and left to dry thoroughly, the length of time depending on the varnish being used. Once dry all the grain fibres remaining loose on the surface will be standing up, and the whole job should now be sanded down with a very fine-grade sandpaper. Following coats should be applied at full strength, rubbing down between each coat until the final coat is applied. The number of coats applied depends on how much spare time you have and whether this runs out before your varnish, but I would recommend at least three coats for a good, hard-wearing finish.

Polyurethane varnish has the advantage over the traditional varnish in that it is relatively quick drying (approximately 4 hours), but it does not soak into the timber so readily and tends more to form a surface skin. Therefore the first coat of Polyurethane must be thinned carefully, according to the manufacturer's instructions, and must be worked well in. When completely dry Polyurethane varnish forms an exceptionally hard, durable finish.

Painting

The most important point to bear in mind when dealing with the subject of toys is that any paint used must be entirely lead-free. With modern manufacturing methods most of the paint sold for domestic use is lead-free, but always check that this is the case before purchasing an unfamiliar brand. Wood primers are perhaps the most likely paints to contain lead so be sure to buy a primer without this ingredient.

All timber to be painted should be thoroughly dry and free from grease and dirt. Bare wood should be sealed with a coat of wood primer before any other painting is done. Following the primer should be an undercoat and finally a topcoat, gloss or otherwise. One or two coats of undercoat can be applied, if required, and this will give a firmer base for the topcoat. Each coat of paint, except the final finishing coat, should be rubbed down lightly with a fine-grade sandpaper, and the surface wiped

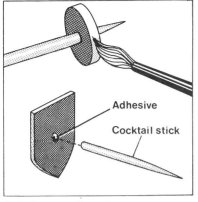

Painting a small component on a holding (cocktail) stick

Suspending a paintbrush temporarily in water

over with a cloth dampened with white spirit to remove dust particles.

Use a good-quality paint brush. As with tools, it is false economy to buy the cheapest brush you can find. These are invariably a good deal weaker in their construction, the head often working loose from the handle and the bristles, usually sparser, regularly adorning your painted surface. Apply the paint evenly, dipping the brush into the paint to a distance of about one-third the length of the bristles, taking not too much and not too little. Excess paint should be eased off the brush against the edge of the paint tin. Work each brush stroke into its neighbour, laying-off away from the wet edge back into the already painted area. Watch out for any small areas you may have missed or for the odd stray bristle; try to catch these before the paint has started to dry. This avoids the risk of unsightly brush marks in the half-set paintwork. Leave all painted components to dry thoroughly before attempting to handle or your efforts may well be wasted.

For the painting of very small items it is best to use a fine, soft artist's brush with either camel or sable hairs. Humbrol enamels are ideal for painting these small parts as they dry quickly and with the majority of colours have a strong pigment, necessitating only one topcoat. With this enamel you can afford to be generous in its application. Flow the paint on to the component part until you have covered the entire surface, then, assuming you have it mounted on a holding stick (see below), turn the stick between your fingers for a minute or two. The enamel will blend into itself over the complete item and give you a really smooth, high gloss finish, without any brushmarks. The part can then be put aside to dry with little risk of any runs spoiling the finish.

Care of brushes

After every painting job the brush should be thoroughly cleaned with white spirit, or turpentine, and then washed in hot soapy water, finally giving it a good rinse in clean water. By taking the trouble to clean your brushes properly after every use, they will last for a long time and give you very good service.

Brushes can be left for a short time in a jar of water, but they should be supported and not left with the bristles bearing the full weight of the brush. Most brushes have a hole drilled through the handle and a short piece of wire pushed through this hole will enable the brush to be suspended across the top of the jar. This hole in the handle is also very handy for hanging up your brushes from a nail or pin. Really old brushes that are clogged-up with old paint but still retain their bristles can be given a new lease of life by a good soaking in paint stripper before being given the soap and water treatment.

Holding the work

With many toys some of the parts to be painted are quite small and therefore difficult to hold whilst painting. Those of you who have ever done any model making will be aware of some of these problems and may well have your own solutions. But for those of you who are new to the game, the following tips may prove useful. Remember, when painting before assembly, not to paint any areas

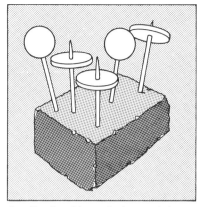

Small painted items drying on their holding sticks in a block of Oasis

that are to receive adhesive.

Small wheels are singularly difficult to hold by themselves. Using a piece of tapered wood or dowel as a makeshift axle, paint each wheel in turn and set aside to dry. If the hole in the wheel is quite small then it can be pressed on to a cocktail stick prior to painting, or a length of thin wire can be inserted through the hole and the wheel painted on the wire. The wire can afterwards be bent into a hook and the wheel hung up to dry. Cocktail sticks can be used as holding sticks with many small items. If the item does not have a handy hole, cut the end of the cocktail stick square, and using just a dab of adhesive, stick it to the back of the component; when the item has been painted and is dry, the stick can be simply broken or cut away from the back. This procedure can also be used on the larger components, using a piece of dowel rod instead of a cocktail stick.

Where you have a lot of small items to paint before assembly, you will have the additional problem of where to put all the cocktail sticks which you have used to support them. A simple and effective method is to push each stick into a block of Oasis. This is the substance sold in florists for flower arranging, but it works equally as well for modelling. Plasticine is another successful alternative, if you can persuade the children to part with enough for your purposes. An old polystyrene packing box is also ideal for this purpose.

The final effect
The finish you give to your toys is going to be critical. It can make or break them visually, so it is worth while spending time and exercising care when you get to this stage. Any toy, whether varnished or painted in gay colours, merits all the skill you can muster and when you finally stand back and look at your finished project you will not be sorry you took the trouble to do the job properly.

Designs to Make

Before you begin please note:

(a) In the materials lists given for each project, all timber has been given its three relevant dimensions. The first two dimensions are the actual stock size of timber required: the last dimension being the maximum length you are likely to require on any particular project. Allowance has been made in the lengths quoted for a little surplus in all instances. Finished dimensions are specified on the accompanying working drawings.

(b) All screws, except some of the smaller sizes, are steel. The very small sizes only being available in brass. All the hinges specified are brass. Quantities are specified in brackets.

(c) With several of the toys, a dowel rod construction has been used. Where a dowel rod performs as an axle, a clearance hole should be drilled to accommodate it, allowing the axle to turn freely. Where a dowel rod is to be a fixed part, the hole drilled to receive it can be the same diameter as the dowel. Bear in mind that dowels vary fractionally in finished size, and it may be necessary to sand the rod down to obtain the required push fit.

(d) All timber components, even though not specifically mentioned in the instruction text, should be rubbed down thoroughly, working through to a fine-grade sandpaper, and obtaining the smoothest finish possible.

Rainbow Spinner

Illustrated in colour on page 54

Materials
Scrap plywood
Fine string
$\frac{1}{4}''$ dia. dowel scraps

This is one of the oldest toys devised for the amusement of children. Since man first invented the wheel and discovered this variation it has been consistently popular. Rainbow-spinner, whizzer, whirler or twirler, it has remained a firm favourite. Its construction is extremely simple yet it continues to provide hours of fun.

CONSTRUCTION
All that is needed is a disc, and this need be no more than three or four inches in diameter. Thin plywood, between $\frac{1}{8}$in. and $\frac{1}{4}$in. thick, is the ideal material. Mark out and cut a disc, but do not lose the centre point. Draw a line through the centre and measure off two points about $\frac{3}{8}$in. on either side of the centre point. Drill a fine hole, about $\frac{1}{16}$in., through each of the two marked points, sand the whole disc to a smooth finish. Thread the string through the two holes and tie the two ends together – the spinner is now completed. As an added refinement, make up two small holding handles from dowel rod.

Variation
To make the spinner buzz, or whine, simply file, or cut, a series of notches all the way round the edge of the disc. The disc should be painted in bright colours for the best effect.

Caveman Rocker

Illustrated in colour on page 23

Materials
$2'' \times 1'' \times 3''$ scrap timber (body)
$2'' \times \frac{5}{8}'' \times 4''$,, ,, (rockers)
$\frac{1}{4}''$ dia. $\times 2''$ dowel scrap (arms, nose)
$\frac{1}{8}''$ dia. $\times 2''$,, ,, (axe handle)

CONSTRUCTION
Mark out, on a piece of timber 2in. by 1in., the shape of the body and include the positions of the arms and the nose. Cut round the body shape with a coping saw and smooth off the head with a flat file. At the base of the body, mark on the positions of the two rockers, and using a round file, cut out the curved area between them.
The arms and nose are made from $\frac{1}{4}$in. dowel rod, so select a drill bit of this size and drill the three holes into the face – these need only be about $\frac{1}{4}$in. deep. To achieve a nice rounded end to the arms and nose, it is best to do the rounding on the complete dowel rod before cutting; first by filing and then by finishing with fine sandpaper. Having cut both the arms and the nose to length, drill a $\frac{1}{8}$in. diameter hole through one of the arms – to take the axe handle. This is made from $\frac{1}{8}$in. dowel rod so check that it is a good push fit through the end of the arm. Apply adhesive to the inside of the three holes in the face and insert the arms and nose, making sure that the hole in the axe arm is vertical. Now, cut out the two rockers from $\frac{5}{8}$in. thick scrap. If you don't have a compass to scribe the curve of the rocker, use the base of a tin, or jar, to draw round. Clamp the two rockers together and file them as a matched pair; this will ensure a really smooth action when assembled. Glue the completed rockers to the base of the body. Finally, cut out the axe head from a piece of scrap, drill a $\frac{1}{8}$in. hole through it, and glue it to its handle and into the arm.

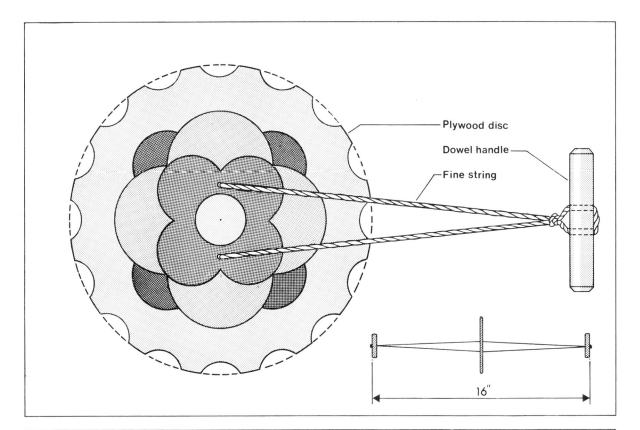

Plywood disc

Dowel handle

Fine string

16"

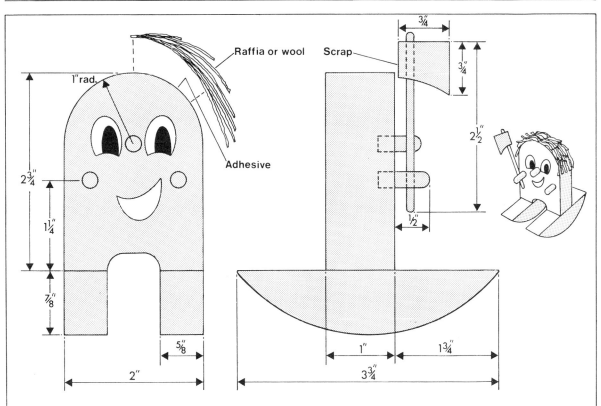

Raffia or wool

Scrap

Adhesive

1" rad.

2¾"

1¼"

⅞"

5⁄8"

2"

¾"

¾"

2½"

½"

1"

1¾"

3¾"

Bead Counter (Abacus)

Illustrated in colour on page 30

Materials
$5\frac{1}{2}'' \times \frac{7}{8}'' \times 1'$ pine (ends)
$\frac{5}{16}''$ dia. $\times 6'$ dowel (rods)
$\frac{3}{4}''$ dia. wooden balls
adhesive

CONSTRUCTION

Using a 30 deg. set square, very carefully mark out the two ends on $5\frac{1}{2}$in. by $\frac{7}{8}$in. timber, accurately plotting the six centres. Cut out both ends and clamp them together, plane off, and sand down, to an exactly matching pair. Now, drill the holes for the six rods through both pieces.

Cut the rods from $\frac{5}{16}$in. dowel, 1ft. long: smooth them down with fine-grade sandpaper. Assemble the structure, and if it is distorted, ease the offending holes to correct the error. There should be ten beads per rod, and all, or any, of the rods, can be used to carry beads. Drill the required number of wooden balls.

An $\frac{11}{32}$nd. bit will give an easy slide fit. Glue three rods to each end and assemble to set, properly aligned. Once dry, slide the two ends apart, add the beads, painted or otherwise, and glue the other ends of the rods. Finally, trim off the surplus rods from the outside.

Flexible Crocodile

Illustrated in colour on page 54

Materials
$2'' \times 1'' \times 9\frac{1}{2}''$ scrap timber (body)
$\frac{1}{4}'' \times \frac{1}{4}'' \times 6''$ ramin (legs)
$\frac{1}{2}''$ dia. $\times 1''$ dowel (wheels)
$\frac{1}{2}''$ upholstery pins (4), string, adhesive

CONSTRUCTION

Body This is cut from scrap timber, 2in. by 1in., cut out to the exact length indicated. Mark on the positions of the dividing lines for the sections, 1–5; carry them right round the timber. Shape the tapered sides of the body first, planing them to the required shape. Start with the head and plane from line No. 1 forwards, and line No. 3 backwards. The sections between these two dividing lines should remain flat-sided for the fixing of the legs and wheels. Now draw the shape of the

crocodile on to the side of the timber, and cut out with a coping saw, excluding, at this stage, the indents along the back. Clean up with a flat file, paying particular attention to the shaping of the head. Re-draw the dividing lines across the top. The indents along the back can now be cut with a $\frac{1}{4}$in. round file, using straight, firm strokes. Reduce the depth of cut as you work towards the tail end. Cut the grooves between the nostrils and eyes with a sharp chisel. Now cut the crocodile into sections using a fine-

toothed saw. File a slight curve across these cut faces, allowing the body to swing when assembled. Finally, drill two holes through each section, as shown on the drawing. Take care to ensure that the exit holes from one section exactly match up to the entry holes in the neighbouring section, otherwise the body will twist when assembled. The sections can now be threaded together. Start with the tail section: coat the ends of the two strings with adhesive and wedge them into the holes with cocktail sticks. When the

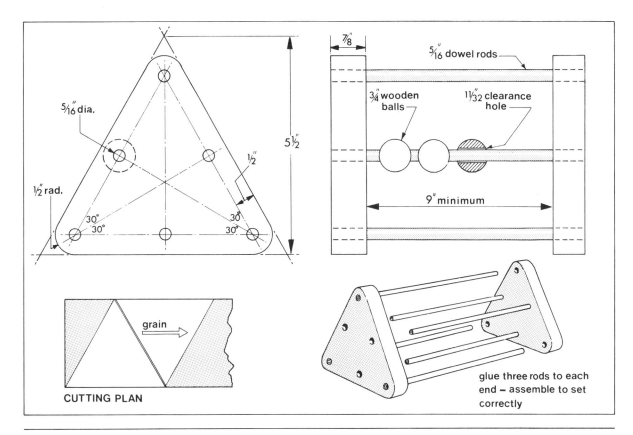

CUTTING PLAN

grain →

5/16" dia.

5/16" dia.

1/2"

1/2" rad.

30° 30° 30° 30°

5 1/2"

7/8"

5/16" dowel rods

3/4 wooden balls

11/32 clearance hole

9" minimum

glue three rods to each end – assemble to set correctly

---

glue has set, cut off the excess stick. Thread right through to the head and finish off by trapping the strings with cocktail sticks, as before. To make the toy a pull-along, drill a small hole in the mouth and insert a further string.

Wheels and legs The legs are cut from $\frac{1}{4}$in. square moulding and each end rounded off, as shown. Drill a pilot hole through each leg for the upholstery pin axles; glue the legs in place. Cut the wheels from $\frac{1}{2}$in. dia. dowel rod, they should be about $\frac{1}{8}$in. thick. Sand them down to a really smooth finish and drill a hole through the centre of each – the hole should be a loose fit over the axle pin. Now, tap the wheels in position with the brass upholstery pins.

Painting Although the crocodile looks fine with a natural finish, he can be painted, as illustrated. If you decide on painting your croc, it should be done before assembly.

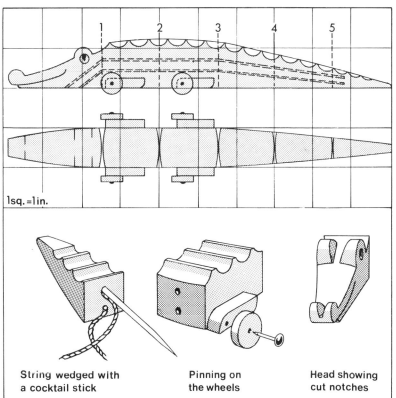

1sq. = 1in.

String wedged with a cocktail stick

Pinning on the wheels

Head showing cut notches

Car Ferry

Illustrated in colour on page 19

Materials

$3'' \times \frac{1}{2}'' \times 3'6''$ pine (hull)
$3'' \times \frac{1}{4}'' \times 6''$ pine (bridgedeck)
$1\frac{1}{4}'' \times 1\frac{1}{4}'' \times 3''$ pine (bridge)
$\frac{3}{4}''$ dia. $\times 2''$ dowel (funnel)
$\frac{3}{16}''$ dia. $\times 2''$ dowel (mast)
$\frac{3}{4}'' \times \frac{1}{2}''$ brass hinges (4)
$\frac{1}{2}''$ No. 1 flathead screws (16)
$1''$ panel pins
adhesive

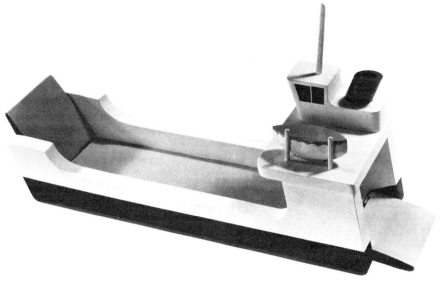

CONSTRUCTION

This craft has been designed to accommodate six, standard-sized, matchbox cars; however, the dimensions can be altered quite easily, if you need to increase the carrying capacity.

Hull This consists of three basic units: the two sides and the main floor, this latter being fitted with a hinged ramp at either end. Both the ramps should be fitted to the floor before the sides are assembled. This is the procedure to follow. Take the 3in. by $\frac{1}{2}$in. timber, mark out and cut, to the overall lengths only, the main hull floor and the two side pieces. Square off both ends of the floor and glue to each a piece of scrap, at least a $\frac{1}{4}$in. thick and long enough to cover the entire end area (this will give the small screws, used on the hinges, a good bite, rather than depending on them holding in the bare end-grain of the floor): when the glue has set, clean off and trim these scrap ends, as necessary. Now, take up the two side lengths, and mark out the exact shape on one of them; the portholes are optional, but if you want to add them, mark these on also. Clamp both pieces together and, using a coping saw and the files at your disposal, carefully cut them out as an exactly matching pair; round off the internal curves with sandpaper wrapped around a dowel rod, drill the holes for the portholes, if required, and clean these out, also using a suitably-sized dowel. Finish off by giving both sides a good rub down with fine-grade sandpaper.

Ramps Mark off the two ramp pieces on 3in. by $\frac{1}{2}$in. timber, but this time with the grain running the other way, i.e. across the width of the boat. Cut them out as one piece, and plane down one edge to a fine taper; sand down, and cut in two. Note that the stern ramp is shorter than that at the bow, so trim this down accordingly and adjust the taper along the edge. Offer up both the ramps to the main floor. Each of them should be a fraction narrower across the width, to provide the clearance necessary for easy operation, when the sides are fitted. Cut the hinge slots in each ramp; they should be about a $\frac{1}{4}$in. from the corners. Fit the hinges in place with $\frac{1}{2}$in. No. 1 screws. It will not be necessary to pilot drill the screwholes as, being small, the screws are unlikely to split the timber. Finally, screw the ramps in place at either end of the main floor. Offer up the sides and with these hand-held in place, check the operation of both ramps to be sure that neither of them binds. If all is

in order, glue and pin on the sides with two or three 1in. pins.

Bridge First, mark out the bridge deck on 3in. by $\frac{1}{4}$in. timber, cut to size and plane the angles on the front and rear edges, matching the angle of the stern as near as possible; round off all the corners, rub down, and glue and pin to the hull assembly. If you intend having the lifeboat on the bridgedeck, drill the two holes for the davits before fixing. Now, using 1$\frac{1}{4}$in. square timber, mark out and cut the bridge to size, shaping it as indicated in the drawing. Drill the $\frac{3}{16}$in. hole for the mast, slightly angling the drill towards the bow and glue in the dowel mast which will now rake towards the stern. Cut the funnel from $\frac{3}{4}$in. dowel rod, drill out the centre and glue it to the bridge. Finally, glue the whole bridge assembly to the deck.

Lifeboat Making this up from scrap is very simple. Trace off the shape from the drawing and transfer it to the scrap timber, at least $\frac{1}{2}$in. thick; cut to size and sand off all round. Then, using a penknife or a sharp chisel, trim it down until you arrive at the hull shape shown in the sketch; sand down thoroughly. Cut the davits from scrap $\frac{1}{8}$in. dowel rod and glue into the bridgedeck.

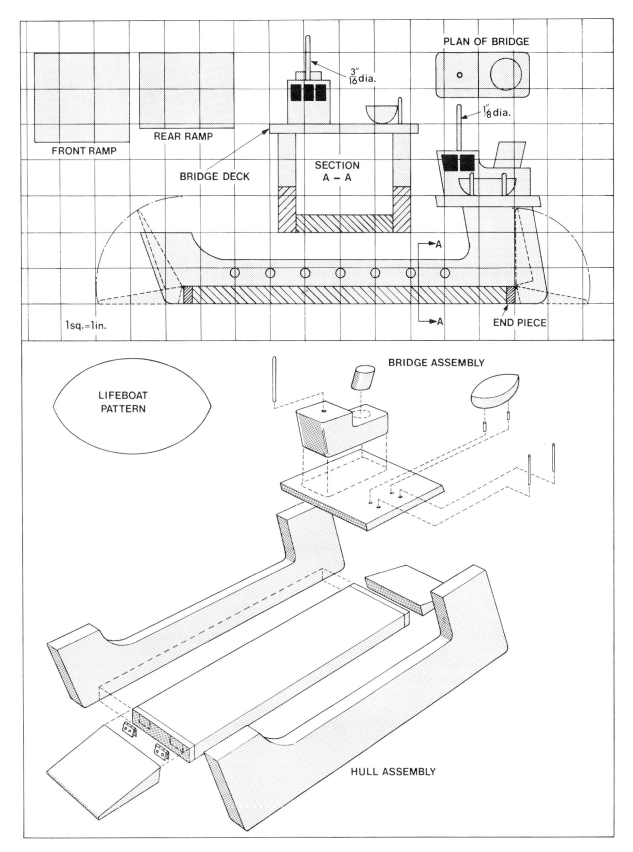

FRONT RAMP

REAR RAMP

BRIDGE DECK

PLAN OF BRIDGE

$\frac{3''}{16}$ dia.

$\frac{1''}{8}$ dia.

SECTION
A – A

A

A

END PIECE

1 sq. = 1 in.

LIFEBOAT
PATTERN

BRIDGE ASSEMBLY

HULL ASSEMBLY

41

Sailing Barge

Illustrated in colour on page 30 and on title page

Materials

$2\frac{1}{4}'' \times \frac{5}{8}'' \times 9''$ pine (hull)
$1\frac{1}{4}'' \times \frac{1}{4}'' \times 1'$ pine (deckhouse, etc.)
$\frac{5}{16}''$ dia. $\times 8''$ dowel (mast)
$\frac{1}{4}''$ dia. $\times 1'$ dowel (spars)
$\frac{1}{8}''$ dia. $\times 1\frac{1}{4}''$ dowel (tiller)
Screw eyes (5 closed)
$\frac{1}{2}''$ brass upholstery pins (2)
fine string, adhesive

CONSTRUCTION

Hull Mark out and cut to size from $2\frac{1}{4}$in. by $\frac{5}{8}$in. timber; round off the corners. The deckhouse, rudder and stempost are all cut from $\frac{1}{8}$in. thick timber, cut to size. Drill the $\frac{1}{8}$in. hole in the rudder for the tiller (made from scrap dowel rod). Glue these items to the hull. Make up the companionway hatch from scrap quadrant and glue in position.

Finally, fit the screw eye to the back of the deckhouse.

Spars Cut the main boom, gaff and bowsprit from $\frac{1}{4}$in. dowel rod, and round the ends off nicely. Drill a fine hole in the outer end of each spar, for the rigging. Pilot drill the bowsprit for two $\frac{1}{2}$in. panel pins, apply adhesive to the base and pin it in position. Fit the screw eyes into the other two spars and set aside.

The mast Cut this, oversize at this stage, from $\frac{5}{16}$in. dowel rod, and round off the top end. Drill the hole for the rigging, and fit the two screw eyes in place. To fix the mast, drill a $\frac{5}{16}$in. hole, at a slight angle, right

through the hull, apply adhesive to the base of the mast and push it right through to the required height. The excess dowel rod poking out of the bottom can now be trimmed off. Open the screw eyes, and fit the spars, squeezing the eyes shut again once the spars are positioned.

Rigging Starting at the bowsprit thread fine string through all the spars, finishing at the eye on top of the deckhouse. Cut the sails from card or coloured cloth. Although the latter is more permanent, card sails can easily be replaced. Finally, cut the two lee-boards from $\frac{1}{4}$in. thick timber and, using brass upholstery pins, pin them in position. They should be left to swing freely.

Simple Animals

Illustrated in colour on page 26

Materials
timber, as required
raffia, or string
adhesive

CONSTRUCTION
The animals can be made from any available timber to any size, but remember that it must be thick enough to enable the animal to stand upright, when cut. Enlarge the shape of your choice from the grid opposite (see chapter 2, page 16); transfer the grid, and plot the shape, down on to your timber. Now, cut out the

shape with a coping saw, sand down really well, paying particular attention to the cut edges. If you intend leaving the timber with a natural finish, paint on the eye before oiling, or varnishing. Next, add the hair and/or tail. The raffia hair on the horse, is inserted into a series of holes drilled down the back of its neck. Put a little adhesive

in each hole and press in the raffia, trimming to length afterwards.

Variation
The shapes have been designed to permit the addition of wheels, and these are simply mounted on loose dowel axles. The wheels should be at least as thick as the timber used for the animal.

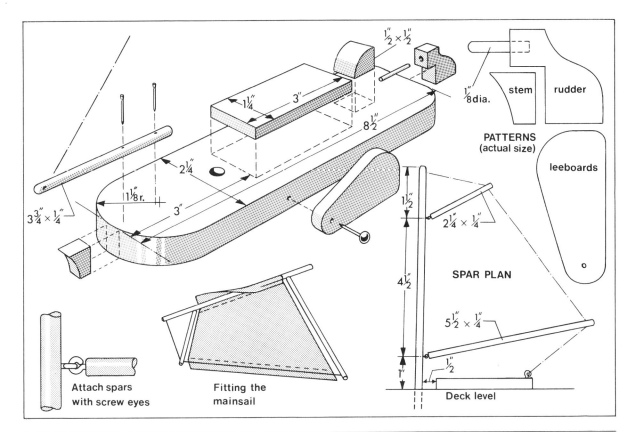

$\frac{1}{2}" \times \frac{1}{2}"$

$1\frac{1}{4}"$

$3"$

$8\frac{1}{2}"$

$\frac{1}{8}"$dia.

stem   rudder

PATTERNS
(actual size)

leeboards

$2\frac{1}{4}$

$1\frac{1}{8}"$r.

$3"$

$3\frac{3}{4}" \times \frac{1}{4}"$

$1\frac{1}{2}"$

$2\frac{1}{4}" \times \frac{1}{4}"$

SPAR PLAN

$4\frac{1}{2}"$

$5\frac{1}{2}" \times \frac{1}{4}"$

$1"$

$\frac{1}{2}"$

Deck level

Attach spars
with screw eyes

Fitting the
mainsail

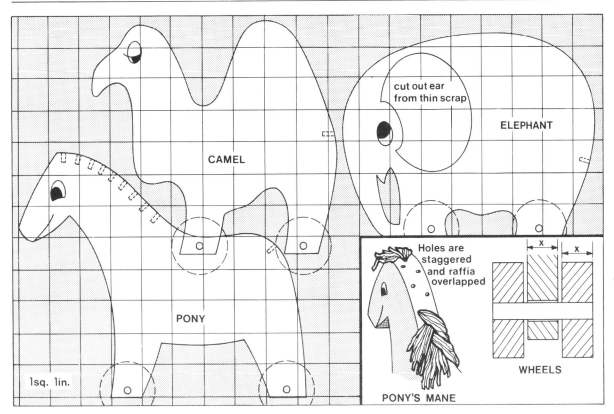

cut out ear
from thin scrap

ELEPHANT

CAMEL

PONY

Holes are
staggered
and raffia
overlapped

x   x

WHEELS

1sq. 1in.

PONY'S MANE

43

Toytown Soldiers

Illustrated in colour on page 19

Materials

Men: $\frac{3}{4}''$ dia. dowel $\Big\}$ length as required
$1'' \times \frac{1}{4}''$

Horses: $1\frac{1}{4}'' \times \frac{5}{8}''$
$\frac{1}{4}''$ dia. dowel $\Big\}$ lengths as required
$\frac{1}{8}''$ dia. dowel
fine string, adhesive

The demise of the lead soldier, in favour of the mass-produced, plastic variety, has left them somewhat devoid of character. These soldiers, being hand-made and hand-painted, will doubtless go part of the way to restoring that lost individualism. The quantity of materials required will depend on how many soldiers you intend to make.

CONSTRUCTION

Infantry

The bodies of all the soldiers are cut from $\frac{3}{4}$in. dowel rod, and each one of them stands 3in. high. First file, and then sand the heads to a nice rounded shape; it is easier to do this before cutting the body from the dowel rod. Next, cut out the notch to form the feet and clean up with a flat file. Drill a small hole, about $\frac{1}{16}$in., half-way up the body, and at right angles to the front, right through to the other side. This hole is for the string used to secure the arms. All the arms are cut from $\frac{1}{4}$in. thick ramin strip. You can either have both arms the same, or you can trace off the pattern and have your soldier carrying a gun. Trim off the lower corners of the arm to form the hand, and drill a small hole through the centre top.

Cavalry

Cut the body of the horse from $1\frac{1}{4}$in.

by $\frac{5}{8}$in. timber; it should be 2in. long. With a sharp chisel, trim off the corners as indicated in the drawing. Now, lay the body on its back and drill the four holes for the $\frac{1}{4}$in. dowel rod legs. Cut the legs slightly overlong and glue in position; once they have set, trim them off to the right length. Now trace off the patterns for the head, neck and tail, transfer your tracing to $\frac{1}{4}$in. thick timber, and cut out. Clean up with sandpaper and glue the head to the neck separately, before glueing the assembly on to the body; finally, glue on the tail. This completes the horse and all that remains is the rider. Once again the body is cut from $\frac{3}{4}$in. dowel rod: he wears a slightly different hat, so cut the dowel to the angle indicated in the drawing. Clean up and set aside for painting. The rider is best painted separately, as once he is glued on to the horse, he will be difficult to paint properly. He has no arms, as such, but can be assembled with a flag or a sword. These are made from $\frac{1}{8}$in. dowel rod and are glued into the top of the horse as indicated.

Crusader *(see page 80)*

Cut the body exactly as for the guardsman but don't round off the top of the head. Now cut out the notch forming the feet, and drill the hole for the arm securing string.

If you want your knight to hold a sword or a spear (these are cut from $\frac{1}{8}$in. dowel rod), drill through the ramin strip, before cutting the arm to length. Once again the arms are cut exactly as those on the guardsman. The shield is simply a door handle, glued and pinned to the right arm.

Painting

A colour guide has been included on the drawings for the various figures. You can, of course, vary the colours of the horses and the knight: the guardsmen, however, cannot be changed – unless you want to start up your own army. Begin by painting the whole body, hands, etc., pink – flesh tone. With this as a base, the other colour bands can be added. The black busbys, the red tunics, the blue trews and the boots. Always start with the lightest colour and progress through to the darkest. Lastly paint on the faces – the expressions will depend on your mood, and your talent. Remember when painting the horses to leave an unpainted area on the back where the rider is to be glued; similarly don't paint the base of the rider. When all the paintwork is thoroughly dry thread fine string through the arms and body, tying off at either side, and sliding the knot as close to the body as you can.

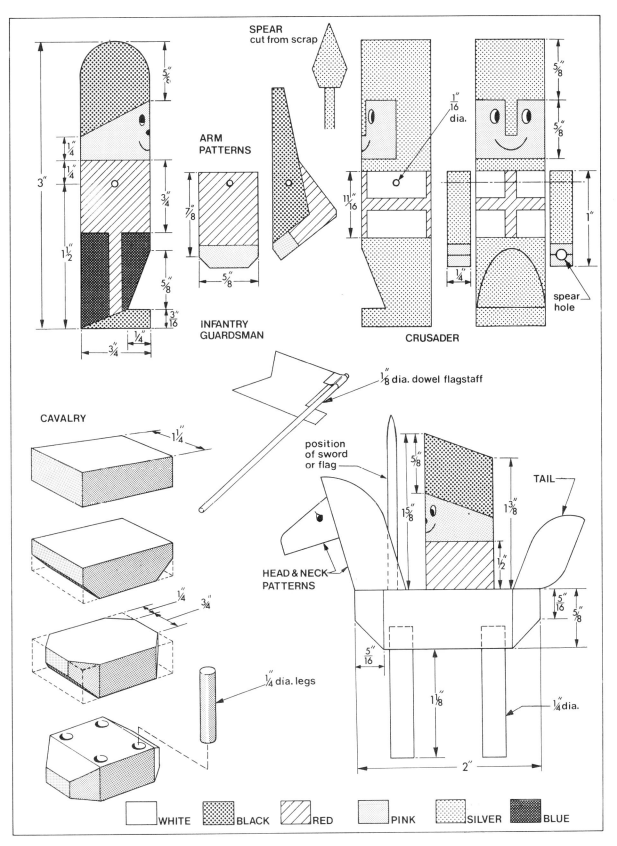

SPEAR
cut from scrap

ARM
PATTERNS

INFANTRY
GUARDSMAN

CRUSADER

spear
hole

$\frac{1}{16}$ dia.

$\frac{1}{8}$" dia. dowel flagstaff

CAVALRY

position
of sword
or flag

TAIL

HEAD & NECK
PATTERNS

$\frac{1}{4}$" dia. legs

$\frac{1}{4}$" dia.

WHITE   BLACK   RED   PINK   SILVER   BLUE

45

Dragster

Illustrated in colour on page 30

Materials

$1\frac{3}{4}'' \times 1\frac{3}{4}'' \times 9\frac{1}{2}''$ pine (body)
$1'' \times \frac{1}{4}'' \times 9''$ ramin (trim)
$\frac{1}{4}''$ dia., $\frac{1}{2}''$ dia., $\frac{3}{16}''$ dia. dowel scraps
$1''$ dia. wooden ball (head)
Fobel plastic wheel kit, $2''$ dia.★
adhesive

CONSTRUCTION

Mark out and cut the body from $1\frac{3}{4}$in. square timber and, using a flat file, round off the leading edge. Sand down the whole body to a good smooth finish. Mark, on both sides, the positions for the axles, and, using a $\frac{1}{4}$in. bit, drill through the body from both sides – the two sets of holes meeting in the middle of the block. Test the fit of the axles and make sure they revolve easily. Next, drill the two holes for the exhaust pipes, $\frac{1}{4}$in. dia., and the

hole for the driver's head-peg, $\frac{3}{16}$in. dia. Cut the exhaust pipes to length and glue them in place. Now cut, from $\frac{1}{2}$in. dowel rod, four washers: drill out the centres so that they slip easily over the axles. These centre holes are best drilled on the complete dowel rod before cutting to length. The side trims can now be marked out and cut to size. These are cut from 1in. by $\frac{1}{4}$in. ramin strip, clean them up and glue them in position. Now make the driver's head from the wooden ball:

drill the hole for the holding peg and make the saw cut for the peak cap – the peak is cut from scrap ply, or card. Cut the two axles to the length required, slide on the washers and the wheels and tap home the hubcaps. Painting should be done before assembly, with the car and driver kept as separate units.

★These wheels are usually white but have been painted to match the livery.

Stunt Flyer

Illustrated in colour on page 19

Materials

$2'' \times 1'' \times 6''$ pine (body)
$\frac{1}{4}'' \times 2'' \times 1'$ ply (wings)
$\frac{3}{4}''$ dia. wooden balls (4)
$\frac{3}{16}''$ dia. $\times 2''$ dowel rod
$\frac{1}{2}''$ panel pins, adhesive

CONSTRUCTION

Body Mark out the side shape, on 2in. by 1in. timber, cut to size and sand down. Next, shape the sides by planing off towards each end, leaving the centre section, where the wing is fitted, square. Trim back, from the cockpit to the tail, with a sharp knife or chisel. Finally, drill the $\frac{3}{16}$in. hole for the pilot's holding peg.

Wings Cut templates of the wing shapes from thin card and draw

round these on to the ply: cut out both the wings and sand well down. Mark the exact position of the wing slot on the body and cut it out. Glue and pin both wings in place, square them up and set aside.

Undercarriage Make up the wheel block from scrap timber and drill a clearance hole for the $\frac{3}{16}$in. axle: glue the block in position. Drill the two ball wheels for their axle, cut this from dowel, overlong at this stage, and glue on one of the wheels.

Slide the axle through the undercarriage block, cut to length and glue on the other wheel. The nose cone, cut from a ball, can either be glued straight on to the body, or you can make up the spinner from thin ply, and fix it in place with a screw axle.

NOTE: Painting should be done before fitting the wheels and pilot.

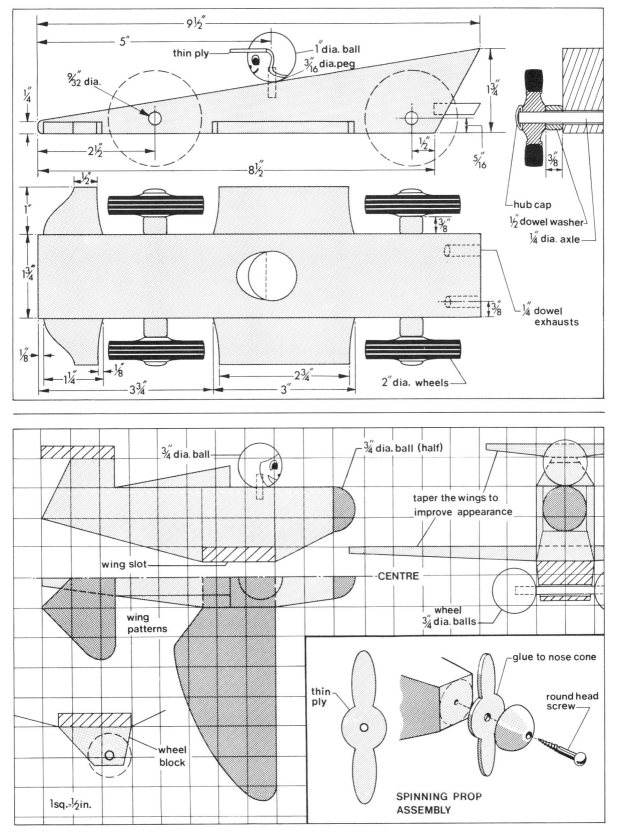

9½"

5"

thin ply

1" dia. ball
³⁄₁₆" dia. peg

⁹⁄₃₂" dia.

¼"

1¾"

2½"

5⁄₁₆"

8½"

½"

½"

hub cap
½" dowel washer
¼" dia. axle

¼" dowel exhausts

1"

1¾"

⅜"

⅜"

⅜"

⅛"

⅛"

1¼"

3¾"

2¾"

3"

2" dia. wheels

¾" dia. ball

¾" dia. ball (half)

taper the wings to improve appearance

wing slot

CENTRE

wing patterns

wheel ¾" dia. balls

wheel block

1 sq.=½ in.

thin ply

glue to nose cone

round head screw

SPINNING PROP ASSEMBLY

Train Set

Illustrated in colour on page 23

Materials

$1\frac{1}{2}'' \times 1\frac{1}{2}'' \times 1'$ pine (rolling stock)
$1\frac{1}{4}'' \times \frac{1}{4}'' \times 1'6''$ pine (chassis)
$\frac{5}{8}''$ dia. $\times 6''$ dowel (chimney, wheels)
$\frac{1}{8}'' \times 2'' \times 1'$ ply scrap (roofs)
$1\frac{1}{8}''$ dia. dowel (boiler)
$\frac{1}{2}''$ brass upholstery pins (20)
screw eyes (4 open – 4 closed)
adhesive

Every little boy, at some time in his life has wanted to play with trains, and some of them continue to do so until their late sixties. Good luck to them say I; however elaborate or simple, trains are fascinating things. This one is of the simple variety and is very easy to make. Painted in primary colours it makes an attractive toy, and with its easily detachable carriages and tender, will keep a child amused for hours.

CONSTRUCTION

The basic construction of the train is very similar to that used for the flexible crocodile on page 38, in that the engine-cab, tender, both the carriages and the guard's van are all shaped as one unit and then sawn into separate parts. Take a piece of timber $1\frac{1}{2}$in. by $1\frac{1}{2}$in. and approximately 1ft. long and plane off both sides as indicated in the drawing. Now make a curve along the top, initially by careful planing and then by sanding smooth; take care not to make this curve too dramatic or you will have trouble when you come to fit on the roof pieces. This completes the basic shaping and you can now start to mark out the individual components. Having done this, use a coping saw to cut out all the windows, the back of the guard's van and the area between the engine-cab and the tender. Smooth out the rounded corners, and the bottoms of the windows with a round file. Give the whole piece a thorough sanding and saw it into the five separate units – clean up all the cut edges. Now make the cuts necessary to complete the tender.

Chassis Cut all these pieces from $\frac{1}{4}$in. by $1\frac{1}{4}$in. timber. These should all be cut $\frac{1}{4}$in. longer than their respective component part, allowing for an overlap of $\frac{1}{8}$in. at each end. Glue each piece of rolling stock to its respective chassis, except for the engine-cab.

Engine The engine boiler is cut from $1\frac{1}{8}$in. dowel rod and is glued and screwed to the engine chassis. Drill the two screw holes and, with these as a guide, drill pilot holes in the boiler. Plane a small flat along the base of the boiler and apply a little adhesive before finally screwing home. The engine-cab can now be glued in position. The funnel is cut from $\frac{5}{8}$in. dowel rod and its base should be shaped with a round file to fit the top of the boiler. Glue in position. All the roof pieces are cut from thin ply; $\frac{1}{8}$in. is ideal, as it will bend across the roof curve easily. Mark out the ply and cut as one long strip before separating it into the four units needed. The roof pieces are glued and pinned into place with $\frac{1}{2}$in. pins; glue alone will not hold them down over the curve.

Wheels For the wheels, cut slices from $\frac{5}{8}$in. dowel rod. They should be about $\frac{1}{8}$in. thick and should be sanded to a smooth finish. Drill a hole through each wheel for the axle and, using upholstery pins, pin them on to the five chassis. The buffers at the rear of the guard's van and the front of the engine are also upholstery pins. The only thing that now remains to be done is the fixing of the screw eyes. You will need four open eyes, and four closed eyes, one pair for each truck. The open eye is best left pointing upwards, as this makes each truck easier to hook and unhook.

Painting can be done as you go along or you can paint the whole thing on completion, leaving only the wheels to be put on afterwards. With this number of wheels to paint, you will find that cocktail sticks will come in very handy as holding sticks.

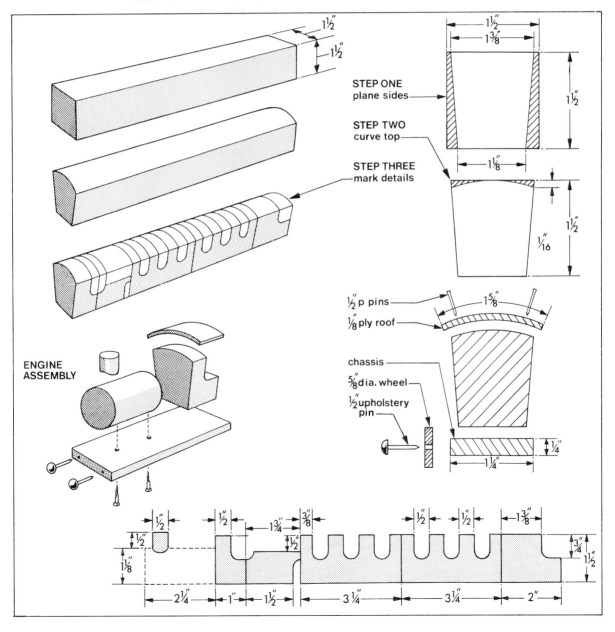

STEP ONE
plane sides

STEP TWO
curve top

STEP THREE
mark details

$1\frac{1}{2}''$

$1\frac{3}{8}''$

$1\frac{1}{2}''$

$1\frac{1}{8}''$

$1\frac{1}{2}''$

$\frac{1}{16}''$

$\frac{1}{2}''$ p pins

$\frac{1}{8}''$ ply roof

$1\frac{5}{8}''$

chassis

$\frac{5}{8}''$ dia. wheel

$\frac{1}{2}''$ upholstery pin

ENGINE
ASSEMBLY

$\frac{1}{4}''$

$1\frac{1}{4}''$

$\frac{1}{2}''$ $\frac{1}{2}''$ $1\frac{3}{4}''$ $\frac{3}{8}''$ $\frac{1}{2}''$ $\frac{1}{2}''$ $1\frac{3}{8}''$

$\frac{1}{2}''$ $\frac{1}{2}''$ $\frac{3}{4}''$ $1\frac{1}{2}''$

$1\frac{1}{8}''$

$2\frac{1}{4}''$ $1''$ $1\frac{1}{2}''$ $3\frac{1}{4}''$ $3\frac{1}{4}''$ $2''$

Noah's Ark

Materials

$3'' \times 2'' \times 3'$ pine (hull)
$1\frac{1}{4}'' \times \frac{1}{4}'' \times 4'6''$ pine (deckhouse, ramp)
$3'' \times \frac{1}{4}'' \times 2'$ pine (roof)
$\frac{1}{2}''$ thick scrap pine (rudder, stempost)
$\frac{1}{4}''$ dia. $\times 3''$ dowel (tiller)
$\frac{1}{4}'' \times 1'6'' \times 6''$ ply (floor)
$\frac{1}{2}''$ panel pins
adhesive (*waterproof*)

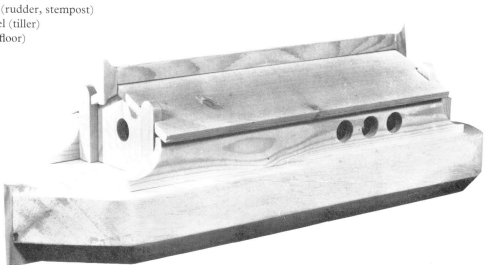

Although this ark has a rather modern-looking rudder, the original probably having a steering oar, my intention was to create a craft that was both attractive and functional in appearance. It can be made either as a proper boat, or it can be fitted with wheels and pulled along. A note of this variation appears below.

CONSTRUCTION

Hull This is made in two halves from 3in. by 2in. timber. Examine the wood carefully, for knots and splits, and having selected the best areas, mark off and cut the two hull lengths: at this stage cut them off square. With both pieces held together, mark on the position of the hold. With your try square, carry these position lines, from the deck, right round to the base of the hull: cut out the hold area from each half. Use your tenon saw to make the down cuts, and then with your coping saw, cut along the length of the hold to link the two down cuts. Clean up the cut faces, if

necessary, with a chisel or flat file, and finish by sanding down thoroughly.

Mark the positions of the slots, for the rudder and the stempost, and cut them out: it is better to cut these undersize, as they can always be eased to fit later. Now, saw the bow angle, from the front back to the side, maintaining a sharp angle at the very front. Cut the stern curve with a coping saw and smooth off with a flat file – also smooth the bow angle where it meets the side of the hull. Finally, glue both halves of the hull together.★

When the assembly has set, mark the position of the bevel round the base, and plane down to your marks. Glue and pin the ply floor, cut from $\frac{1}{4}$in. sheet, and when dry, bevel to match the hull. The rudder and stempost can now be cut from $\frac{1}{2}$in. thick timber. They should be sanded down really well, bringing up the end grain to a good finish. Drill a $\frac{1}{4}$in. hole through the top of the rudder, to take the dowel rod tiller; this

should be a good push fit. Glue both the rudder and stempost in position, easing the slots if necessary. The hull is now complete.

Deckhouse Mark off, and cut from $\frac{1}{4}$in. by $1\frac{1}{4}$in. timber, the two side pieces. To match both sides, clamp them together and cut out the shaped ends with a coping saw, finishing off with a piece of sandpaper wrapped around a thick dowel rod. Now drill the holes for the windows, clamping each side, in turn, to a solid piece of scrap to avoid splitting the thin timber: drill right through into the scrap. Sand out the holes and give the sides a final sanding. The ends of the deckhouse are also cut from $\frac{1}{4}$in. by $1\frac{1}{4}$in. timber, each end being three vertical pieces, glued together side by side. Cut the three pieces long enough to accommodate both ends, glue them together and set aside to dry. When dry, sand thoroughly and mark on the two end elevations with their details: cut out and give them both

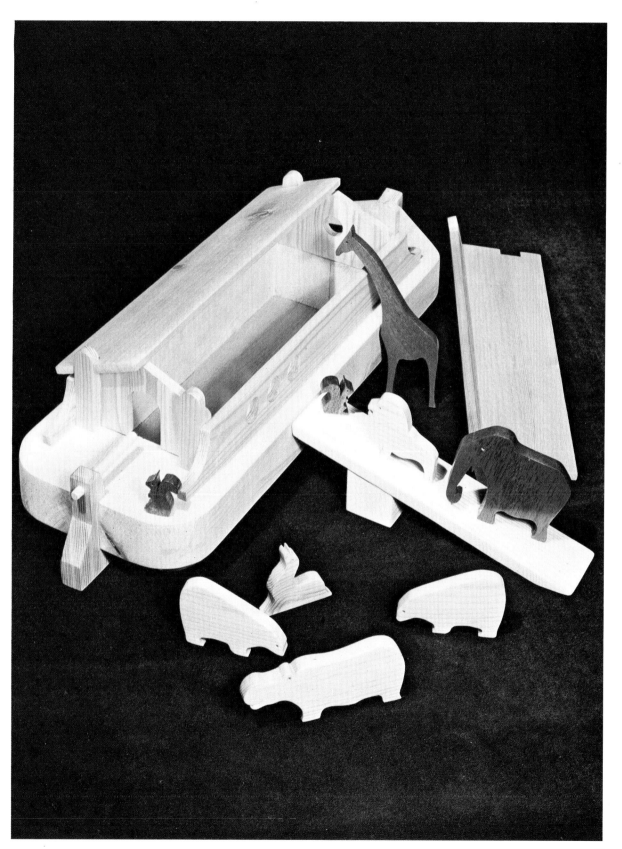

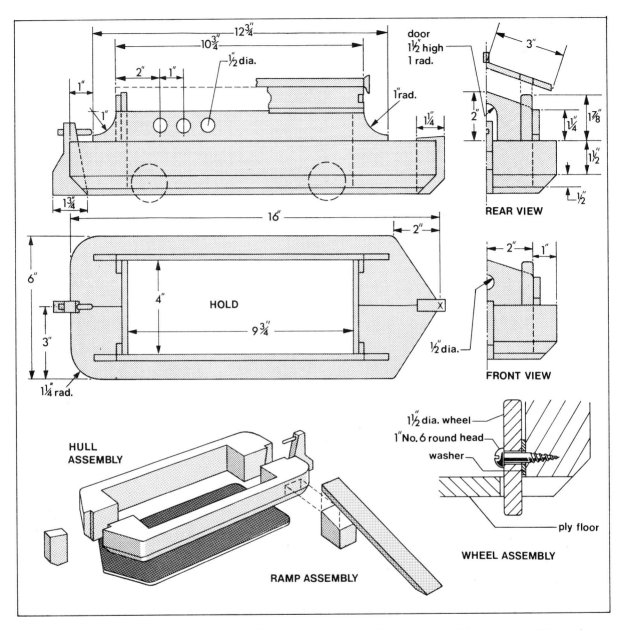

a final sanding. Mark their positions on the side walls and, after pre-pinning, glue and pin the deckhouse assembly together. Take care when pinning the door end to slip the door opening over the lip of a table and then tap in the pins – the table takes the strain. Finally, check the completed deckhouse, for fit, on the hull, and glue the two assemblies together.

Roof supports These are cut from $\frac{1}{4}$in. by $1\frac{1}{4}$in. timber: cut this down

the middle, plane off the sawn edge, cut to length and round off the tops.

Roof Mark off and cut out the two roof pieces from $\frac{1}{4}$in. by 3in. timber. Then, taking a light cut with every stroke, plane off the ridge bevels on each piece: check the two roof halves over the deckhouse as you go. Glue the roof supports in place, at one end of the deckhouse only. Lay the roof pieces against these supports and mark off the correct position of the holding slots. Repeat this

process for both ends of the roof: glue the second pair of roof supports in place.

Carefully cut out the slots in each roof half, cutting them undersize and easing them out to fit snugly over their respective pair of supports. They should have a nice easy fit without being sloppy. A sloppy fit will cause a wide gap along the ridge line. Finally, cut out the ridge beam and the end pieces from scrap, and glue them to one half of the roof only.

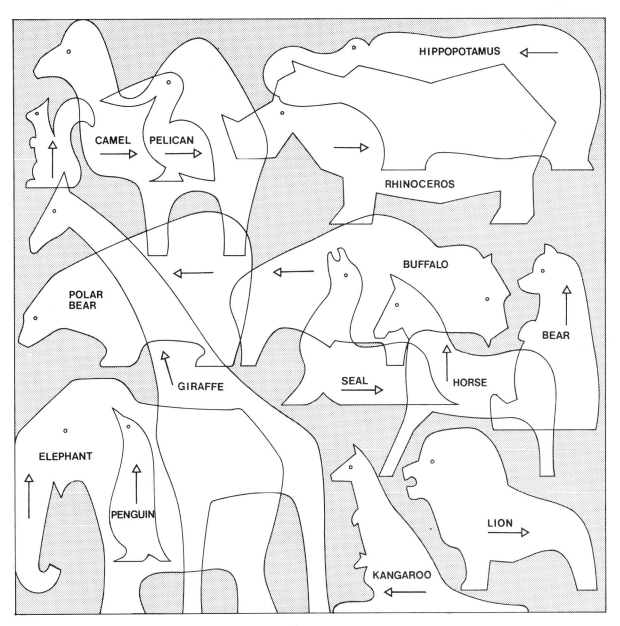

Ramp Cut from $\frac{1}{4}$in. by $1\frac{1}{4}$in. timber and file the bevel at each end. Glue the support block (cut from scrap) in position. Sand thoroughly.

Variation

*If you decide to fit wheels to the ark these must be fitted before the two hull halves are glued together. The wheels are held in place with screw axles, and should be placed so that they project below the level of the hull by at least $\frac{1}{2}$in. This clearance allows for the additional thickness of the floor. Once the wheels are fitted, the two hull halves can be glued together. The floor should be measured to fit the base of the hull exactly. It will need to be bevelled separately to match the hull. Lay the floor against one pair of wheels and mark the positions for the wheel slots; repeat for each side of the floor. The slots should be large enough for the wheels to turn freely when the floor is fitted. Finally, cut out the wheel slots, and glue and pin the floor to the hull.

Animals

Trace off the shapes of the animals from the pattern above and transfer on to $\frac{1}{4}$in. thick timber. Make sure you follow the direction of the grain, as indicated. If you intend making two of each, clamp two thicknesses of timber together, and cut them out as a matching pair. Clean up thoroughly, with sandpaper, using dowels to suit the animal's shape. Finally, drill the $\frac{1}{16}$in. holes for the eyes.

Puppet

Illustrated opposite with the Flexible Crocodile, Rainbow Spinners and the Trolley

Materials

scrap timber (body, hands & feet)
$\frac{5}{16}$″ dia. × 1′ dowel (limbs)
$1\frac{1}{2}$″ dia. wooden ball (head)
screw rings (19), cotton thread

CONSTRUCTION

There are no fixed dimensions for a puppet: the drawing gives only the approximate proportions for an average figure.

Body This is cut from a small length of 2in. by 1in. scrap timber. Using a sharp penknife and the files at your disposal, shape the waist, back and the slope of the shoulders. Cut the corners where the legs are attached at an angle. Clean up the whole body with sandpaper.

Limbs These are all made from $\frac{5}{16}$in. dowel rod, two pieces for each of the four limbs: upper arm, lower arm, thigh and lower leg. The hands and feet are cut from scrap timber and the drawing shows their basic shape: they should be glued to their respective limb sections. The remaining ends of all limb pieces should now be nicely rounded off. The joints are made with small screw eyes, the smaller the better – if still functional. For this reason screw rings are probably better. These are usually smaller than the standard screw eye and come attached to a small circlip which should be removed. The screw eyes can now be fitted to each limb, and the limbs to the body, opening up and closing back the eyes as necessary. All the joints should operate freely without obstruction.

The head is made from a wooden ball. It should be roughly in proportion to the body, but if you err on the large side it will have the advantage of adding more character to the finished puppet. Connect this, as before, with screw eyes. Don't forget the eye in the top of the head for the main holding thread.

Finishing off Paint the hands, feet and head as desired, and varnish the rest of the body. Once the head has been painted you can attach the hair and moustache. Our puppet has a large nose made from a piece of dowel, glued on before painting. Clothing the figure will depend on what scraps of material your wife possesses but whatever is available it should not be too heavy, or the puppet will not be able to move freely.

Finally, attach thin cotton, or nylon thread to the relevant joints: these are best lightly sewn to the clothing. The drawing indicates the positions of the threads; head, elbows, hands, knees and feet, this last item being optional. The hands will need to be drilled with a small hole for their holding threads. To manipulate the puppet make up the cross structure illustrated, from scrap wood and attach the threads as indicated. With a little practice your puppet will soon be performing incredible feats of acrobatics.

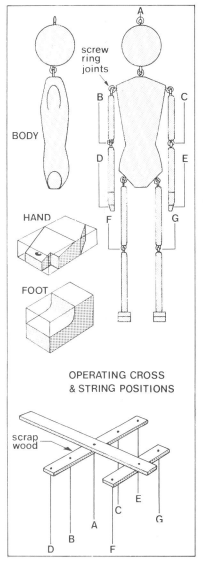

BODY

HAND

FOOT

OPERATING CROSS
& STRING POSITIONS

screw ring joints

scrap wood

55

Fire Engine

Illustrated in colour on page 30

Materials

$3\frac{3}{4}'' \times \frac{7}{8}'' \times 1'$ pine (chassis)
$2'' \times \frac{1}{2}'' \times 1'$ pine (wheels)
$1\frac{3}{4}''$ cube   pine (engine)
$1\frac{3}{4}'' \times \frac{5}{16}'' \times 3'$ pine (bodywork, ladders)
$1\frac{1}{4}'' \times 1\frac{1}{4}'' \times 6''$ pine (seat, swivel block)
$\frac{3}{8}''$ dia. $\times 8''$ dowel (axles)
$\frac{1}{4}''$ dia. $\times 6''$ dowel (pivot spindle)
$\frac{3}{16}''$ dia. $\times 4'$ dowel (ladder rungs)
$\frac{1}{8}''$ dia. $\times 1'$ dowel (holding pegs)
$1''$ dia. wooden balls (2) (lights)
fine string, adhesive

This design can be easily adapted to make many other types of vehicle. The standard chassis and engine unit are common to all,* only the body structure being changed. The vehicle is assembled using a simple system of wooden holding pegs. In all cases these must be a good push fit. The fire engine can be made either with, or without, the extension ladder.

CONSTRUCTION

Chassis Mark out and cut to length from $\frac{7}{8}$in. by $3\frac{3}{4}$in. timber, and cut out the corners for the front wheels. Mark the positions of the four axles, cut from $\frac{3}{8}$in. dowel rod, and drill the holes for these in the sides of the chassis. Cut the axles, overlength, and glue them in position. Finally, drill the hole at the back for the $\frac{1}{4}$in. dowel swivel-spindle.

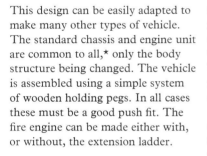

Wheels These are 2in. diameter and $\frac{1}{2}$in. thick. Mark them out and cut carefully with a coping saw, filing and sanding them to a nice round finish. Test each wheel on the axles and mark the positions of the holding pegs; note that the front axle has two sets of pegs, the wheel aligning with the chassis. Drill the $\frac{1}{8}$in. holes for the holding pegs in each axle.

Engine Mark out and cut the engine from a $1\frac{3}{4}$in. cube. Next, mark out

and cut the fire-wall and mudguards from $\frac{5}{16}$in. by $1\frac{1}{4}$in. timber. Round off the top two corners of the fire-wall and glue this, and the engine block, to the chassis: replace the front wheels and, allowing a good clearance, glue on the mudguards.

Cab Mark out and cut the two sides from $\frac{5}{16}$in. by $1\frac{1}{4}$in. timber. Clamp them together, whilst shaping, to ensure a good matching pair. Now, glue two strips of $\frac{5}{16}$in. by $1\frac{1}{4}$in. timber together, to make up the back wall. When set, cut to shape, again rounding off the top corners. Cut the seat from $1\frac{1}{4}$in. square timber, and glue the whole cab assembly together. Before gluing it to the chassis, drill the $\frac{1}{4}$in. hole for the steering column, close up to the fire-wall and at a slight angle. Now, glue the cab to the chassis.

Bumper assembly Cut the bumper from $\frac{1}{4}$in. thick scrap and round off the ends, as shown. Drill the two holes for the headlights and glue the bumper to the chassis. The lights are made from two 1in. diameter wooden balls. Cut these, not quite in half (see sketch), and drill the hole for the holding peg in the base of each. Glue a short length of rod into each light and glue in place on the bumper.

Steering column This is $\frac{1}{4}$in. dowel rod; cut it overlength, and after checking in position on the chassis, cut exactly to length. Make the 1in. diameter wheel from scrap (if you intend having the extension ladder, cut two wheels to this size) and drill the centre to fit easily over the column. Mark the positions of the two holding pegs and drill as before. Glue the finished column into the chassis.

Ladder assembly Cut the swivel-block from $1\frac{1}{4}$in. square timber. Drill the hole for the $\frac{1}{4}$in. dowel spindle, in the centre of the base. Cut this spindle long enough to project right through the chassis and glue it into the block. Mark the position of the holding peg and drill as before. Finally, drill the hole for the ladder pivot-spindle in the position indicated.

Lower ladder Mark out and cut from $\frac{5}{16}$in. thick timber. Each side is $\frac{1}{2}$in. wide. Mark the positions of the 12 rungs, cut from $\frac{3}{16}$in. dowel rod, and drill the holes for these through both pieces at the same time. Insert the rungs, cut over-length, and test fit on the swivel-block. To get the ladder nice and straight, press the two sides together over a piece of scrap, slightly wider

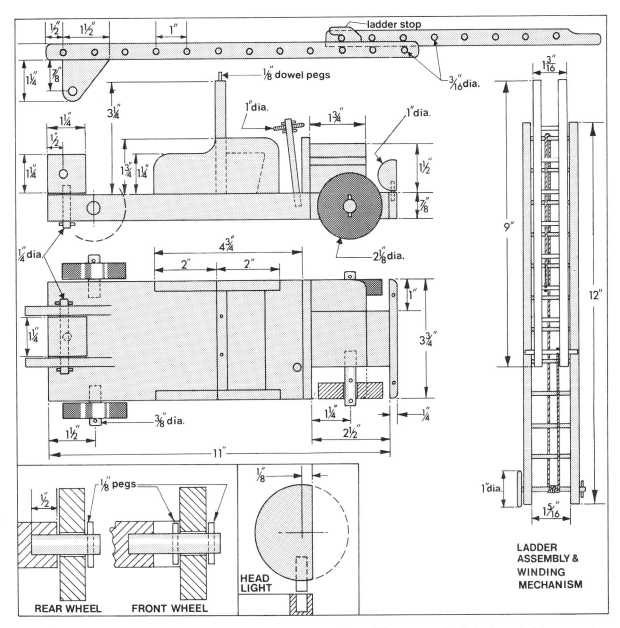

than the swivel-block (see sketch). Glue in the rungs and, once dry, clean off the surplus dowel ends. (If you are fitting the extension ladder, leave out the bottom rung at this stage.)

Make up the two pivot pieces from scrap, drill the pivot holes and glue to the ladder. Finally, cut the pivot spindle and check the pivot action. Drill the spindle for its holding pegs.

Upper ladder Repeat procedure as for lower ladder. But leave the bottom rung long enough to slide up the sides of the lower ladder.

Check that the two ladders operate smoothly together and do not bind. Make up the two ladder stops from scrap, and test that the lowest rung on the upper ladder enters and leaves them smoothly, when hand-held in place. Glue the stops to the lower ladder and test the two ladders together, once more. Finally, make up the turning handle and fit it through the lower ladder. Drill a smaller hole through this rung and make up a peg from a cocktail stick. Using a fine string, thread up the two ladders and the winding mechanism. Be sure to make the string nice and tight, for smooth operation.

*The exception to the chassis dimension given, would occur in, for instance, an omnibus, the length depending on the number of seats.

57

Fold-away Fort

Materials

$\frac{1}{4}'' \times 4' \times 3'6''$ Gaboon ply (main structure)
$2\frac{1}{4}'' \times \frac{1}{2}'' \times 11'$ pine (box base)
$\frac{1}{4}''$ dia. $\times 4''$ dowel (winch barrel)
$1\frac{1}{4}''$ No. 6 flathead screws (16)
$\frac{3}{4}''$ No. 6 flathead screws (12)
$\frac{1}{4}''$ No. 0 flathead screws (8)
$2\frac{1}{2}'' \times \frac{3}{4}''$ brass hinges (2)
$\frac{1}{2}'' \times \frac{1}{2}''$ brass hinges (2)
$\frac{1}{2}''$ panel pins, adhesive, swing-hook latch

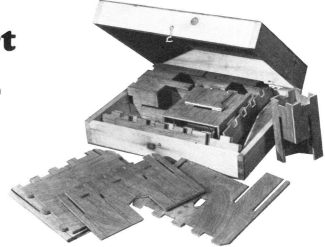

When completely assembled the fort measures 28in. by 19in. by 10in., but can be packed away into a box measuring 13in. by 17in. by 5in. This contains all the various parts of the fort: turrets, walls, gatehouse, ramp and main tower (this being the only structure that needs dismantling before packing). When open, the box forms a solid base on to which all the parts are fitted.

CONSTRUCTION

Study the plans carefully, particularly the cutting plan, which has been worked out to give the minimum of waste. It is drawn on a grid, one square equalling $\frac{1}{2}$in., from which the exact dimensions of each part are taken. Mark out and cut the ramp pieces and odd walls, etc., which interfere with the strips marked on the cutting plan. Now, mark out and cut all the items on strip 1, leaving the base as one piece. Cut these items to their maximum size, leaving all slots, doors and battlements for later. Repeat this procedure for all four strips, cleaning up all the rough edges as you go. All parts should be pre-pinned when assembling.

Base The sides of the base are cut from $2\frac{1}{4}$in. by $\frac{1}{2}$in. timber. Mark off and cut to length. Both the base frames are butt-jointed, glued and screwed together (see page 22, chapter 2). Pilot drill two holes, to take a $1\frac{1}{4}$in. No. 6 screw, in each

end of the front and back frame pieces; countersink them. Glue and screw the two frame assemblies together. Align the hinge-bearing struts, clamp them together and mark the positions of the hinges. Chisel out the hinge slots and fit them, with the cramps in place; this guarantees a good fit when the box is closed. Test fold the box and re-clamp. Cut the base board in two and, without altering the relationship of the two halves, lay them in position on the box frame; check for fit. Now, glue and pin, one at a time, the inside edges of the base boards along the centre joint. Test fold, and re-clamp: lifting each board in turn, squeeze in glue, and pin all round, squaring up, as you go. Finally, fit the latch hook.

Main tower Take the five panels of the tower assembly and cut out all the slots, windows, etc. If you decide to fit a balcony, also cut out the tab-holes for this. The long slots are cut with a tenon saw, and finished off with a fret saw, giving a nice true cut. Check the slots and tab-holes with scrap ply, to see that they are a nice easy fit, it is better to have them a little tight to start with, as they can be eased to the right size with a flat file. DO NOT TRY TO FORCE ANY SLOT or you may split the ply. Assemble, and adjust if necessary.

Turrets Take the first set of five

panels and cut out all the slots, battlements, etc. Note that on the turrets the wall slots are only 2in. high. Glue and pin the two narrow sides to the floor and then add the other two sides. Repeat this procedure for all four turrets.

Gatehouse Cut out all the slots, battlements, etc. Assemble by gluing and pinning the end pieces to the two floors, then the front wall and finally the back wall. Cut out the drawbridge and bevel the wall edge, giving it a downwards tilt to the ramp, and fit the small hinges to the upper face, one at each end. Lay the gatehouse on its back, and screw on the drawbridge. Close it up and drill a small hole in each outer corner, continuing straight through the gatehouse wall. These holes will take the lifting cords. Construct the winch from scrap (see sketch) and glue in position.

Ramp Glue and pin the end piece to the base, and fit the two sides. To achieve the curve over the hump, file the two angles on the sides to a curve, lay the top of the ramp in place, and mark the start of the curve; then, rolling the top piece over the hump, mark the end of the curve. Make a series of saw-cuts between these two marks, half-way through; the top will now fold over the hump quite easily. Try this on a piece of scrap first. Alternatively, fit the top as two separate pieces.

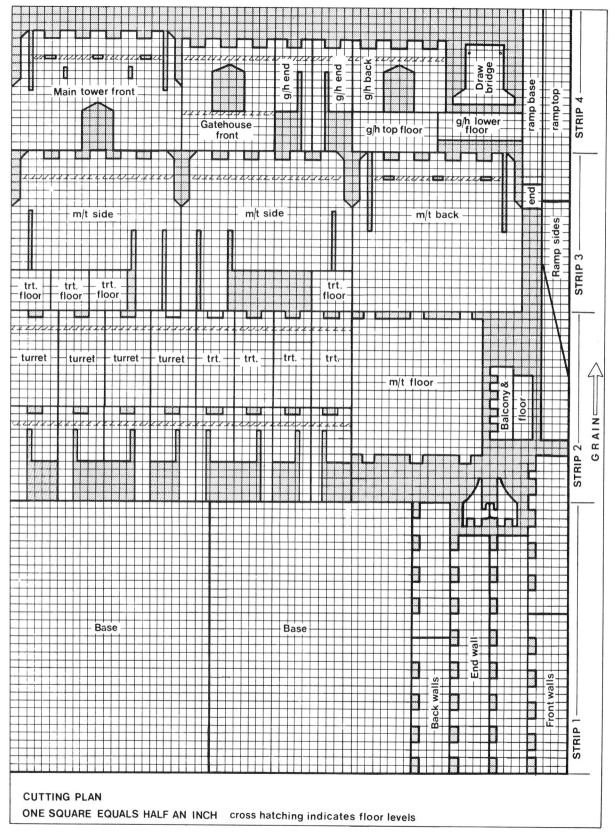

CUTTING PLAN

ONE SQUARE EQUALS HALF AN INCH   cross hatching indicates floor levels

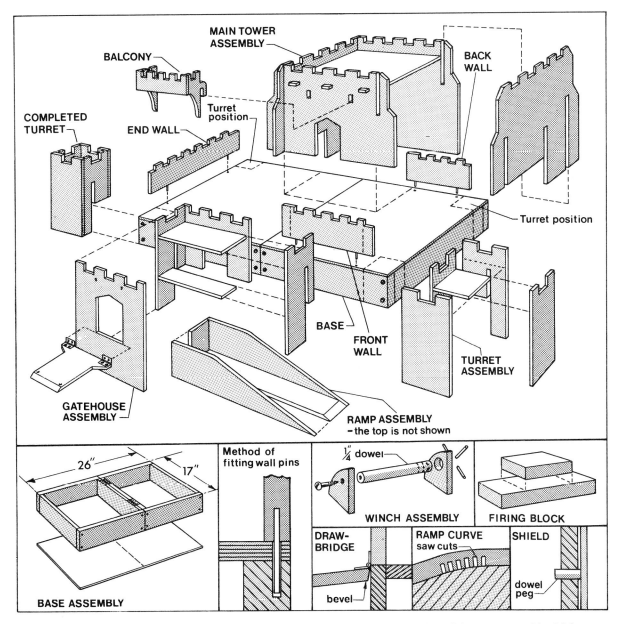

MAIN TOWER ASSEMBLY

BALCONY

BACK WALL

Turret position

COMPLETED TURRET

END WALL

Turret position

BASE

FRONT WALL

TURRET ASSEMBLY

GATEHOUSE ASSEMBLY

RAMP ASSEMBLY – the top is not shown

26"

17"

BASE ASSEMBLY

Method of fitting wall pins

¼" dowel

WINCH ASSEMBLY

FIRING BLOCK

DRAW-BRIDGE

bevel

RAMP CURVE saw cuts

SHIELD

dowel peg

Walls Note the positions of the battlements on the cutting plan. All the walls have a 'high' where they meet a structure, dropping down to 2in. only where they enter the turrets: in all other cases they are 2½in. high. Cut out and sand off rough edges. The walls, when fixed into the base, act as the anchor for the other components (see sketch). Cut the heads off some wire nails, about $\frac{1}{16}$ in. diameter, and drill two slightly smaller holes in the base of each wall. Push the nails into

the wall. Don't hammer them. Press the wall on to the base to mark the position of the anchor holes. Drill these slightly larger than the nails and drop in the wall.

Balcony Lightly pin the assembly together and test fit on the main tower. If it fits properly, glue and pin the assembly together.

Finishing off Completely assemble the whole fort and check that everything fits accurately and the

slots slide apart smoothly. Make up the firing blocks from scrap (see sketch). The shields, shown in the photo on page 58, add a splash of colour to the structure, and are fitted after the fort is painted. Drill through the wall and glue the shield in place with a dowel peg (see sketch). For a rough-painted surface, mix fine sand, or sawdust, with the paint. Alternatively, give the fort two coats of paint and sprinkle on sawdust while the first coat is still wet.

Doll's House

Materials

$\frac{1}{4}'' \times 4' \times 4'$ plywood (main structure)
$3'' \times \frac{1}{2}'' \times 3'6''$ pine (side walls)
$1'' \times \frac{5}{8}'' \times 2'6''$ pine (corner posts)
$1'' \times \frac{1}{4}'' \times 9'$ ramin (roof beams, treads)
$\frac{5}{8}'' \times \frac{1}{2}'' \times 4'$ pine (support beams)
$\frac{3}{4}'' \times \frac{3}{4}'' \times 2'$ pine (ridge spar)
$1\frac{1}{2}'' \times 1\frac{1}{2}'' \times 1'$ pine (chimney)
$\frac{1}{4}'' \times \frac{1}{4}'' \times 3'$ ramin (door drames)
$3'' \times \frac{1}{8}'' \times 3'$ spruce (shutters, window frames, etc.)
$1\frac{1}{4}''$ No. 6 flathead screws (10)
$\frac{1}{2}''$ No. 6   ,,   ,,   (2)
$\frac{1}{4}''$ No. 0   ,,   ,,   (40)
$\frac{1}{2}'' \times \frac{1}{2}''$ brass hinges (10)
$\frac{1}{2}''$ panel pins
adhesive, thin card

For the doll's house illustrated, I have chosen a design based on a typical Swiss cottage. This style of house gives ample opportunity for the introduction of attractive features such as balconies and shutters, items that are easy to make yet give the house a much more interesting appearance. Also, the choice of colours open to the builder is more varied than that facing the builder of a Tudor cottage. A cursory glance at the photo opposite, may indicate that there are a lot of complex shapes and details to worry about. A closer examination of both the picture, and the plans, will show that the construction is relatively easy and the decoration simple to achieve.

CONSTRUCTION

Base Mark this out on $\frac{1}{4}$in. ply and cut to size. Sand down the top surface at this stage; all the later operations are additions to the base and, once assembled, effective sanding will be very difficult. Now, mark the positions of the two main gable walls at each end. The side walls can now be marked off, on 3in. by $\frac{1}{2}$in. timber, and cut to size. Glue and pin these on the base.

End elevations Carefully mark out both the end walls, and the centre dividing wall, on $\frac{1}{4}$in. ply, and cut them out. Clamp all three pieces together and plane off the cut edges to make an exactly matching set. Do not cut the dividing wall in half at this stage. Working from centre lines, drawn from the gable peaks, mark on all the details such as doors, windows, main beam slots and decorative elements (see pattern drawing on page 66). Now, use your fret saw to cut out these items – and don't forget to save the doors. Clean up all the cut edges and corners with a flat file. The holes for the main floor beams should initially be cut undersize, and eased to fit the beams, if necessary. They must provide a good push fit and not be at all sloppy. Cut both the beams to length from $\frac{5}{8}$in. by $\frac{1}{2}$in. timber (see pattern drawing, for the ends). Now, temporarily, pin the two end walls to the base assembly, drop in the centre dividing wall, and check the alignment of the main beams. If they are at all distorted the beam holes will have to be trimmed accordingly: dismantle the assembly.

Corner posts These are cut from 1in. by $\frac{5}{8}$in. timber. Mark off and cut four to length (see pattern drawing). Position each post, in turn, against the end walls; clamp the post and wall together, and drill two holes, large enough to take the shank of a $1\frac{1}{4}$in. No. 6 screw, through both items: countersink the holes in the posts only. If the corner posts are to have fancy edges, now is the time to cut them, as once positioned it will be impossible. Now, glue and screw the four posts, with the end walls sandwiched between them, to the side walls on the base assembly. Don't forget to glue along the base of each wall before screwing the posts home. Turn the whole assembly upside-down and pin through the base into the end walls. To be sure of hitting the target, draw the wall positions on the reverse side of the base.

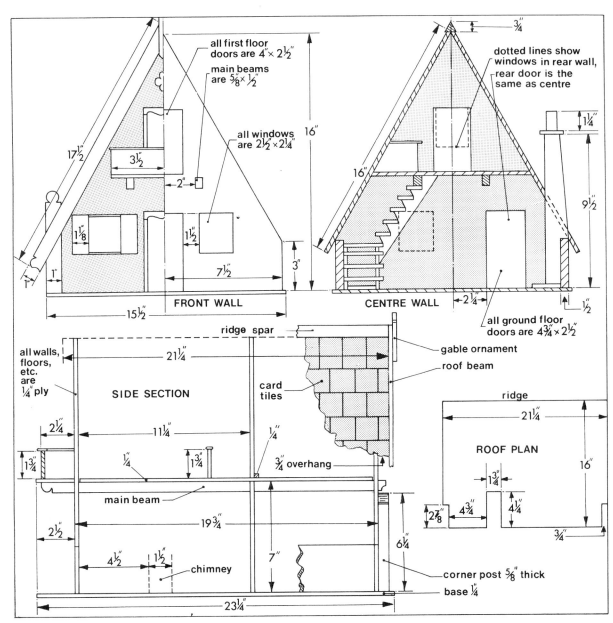

all first floor doors are 4" × 2½"

main beams are ⅝" × ½"

all windows are 2½" × 2¼"

FRONT WALL

17½"

3½"

2"

1⅛"

1½"

1"

1"

7½"

15½"

16"

3"

CENTRE WALL

dotted lines show windows in rear wall, rear door is the same as centre

¾

1¼"

16"

9½"

2¼

½"

all ground floor doors are 4¾" × 2½"

ridge spar

SIDE SECTION

all walls, floors, etc. are ¼" ply

21¼

card tiles

gable ornament

roof beam

2¼"

11¼"

¼"

1¾"

1¾"

¼"

¾" overhang

main beam

19¾"

2½"

4½"

1½"

chimney

7"

6¼

corner post ⅝" thick

base ¼"

23¼"

ROOF PLAN

ridge

21¼"

16"

1¾"

2⅞"

4¾"

4¼"

¾"

Dividing wall Cut this in half, making two saw cuts, ¼in. apart, to remove the thickness of the first floor from the overall height. Glue and pin the ground floor half of the dividing wall within the base assembly; pin first through the side walls, and then up through the base. Check the main beams for fit, once more, and glue in place.

Staircase This is made as two flights. The first flight consists of a pair of sides and a base; cut these from

¼in. ply, and glue and pin together. All the stair treads are cut from 1in. by ¼in. ramin; cut to length and glue to the first flight assembly, excluding the landing strips at this stage. When set, glue the whole assembly within the house – making sure that it fits snugly against the dividing wall and the side wall. Mark out, and cut from ¼in. ply, the two tread supports for the second flight. Check the fit of the inner support against the centre dividing wall – it should be a snug

fit between the first flight of stairs and the main beam. If any adjustment is necessary it will need to be made to both supports. Glue stair treads to the second flight tread supports, and when set, glue the second flight in position to the dividing wall, the first flight and the main beam. Finally, glue on the landing treads.

Upper floor Mark out and cut from ¼in. ply, marking the position of the upper dividing wall. Check that the

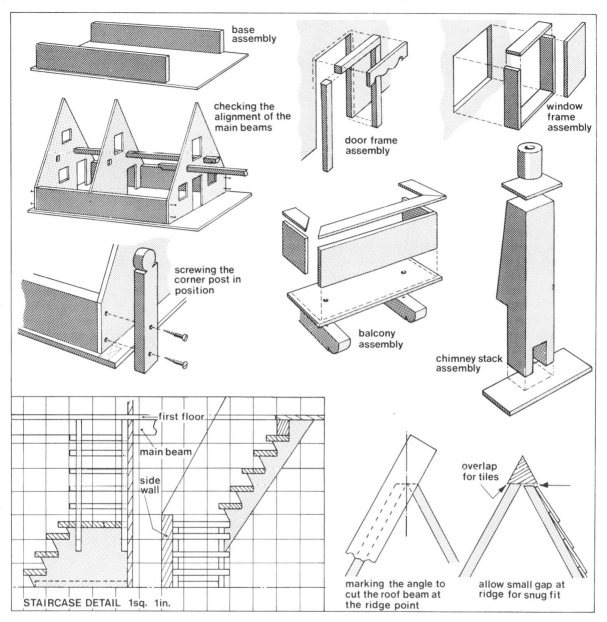

base
assembly

checking the
alignment of the
main beams

door frame
assembly

window
frame
assembly

screwing the
corner post in
position

balcony
assembly

chimney stack
assembly

first floor

main beam

side
wall

STAIRCASE DETAIL 1sq. 1in.

marking the angle to
cut the roof beam at
the ridge point

overlap
for tiles

allow small gap at
ridge for snug fit

whole floor has an easy slide-and-lift fit between the two end walls. With the floor in place, mark the area of the staircase-well on the underside and cut out: the floor should extend to the edge of the main beam, where it meets the staircase, but should not overlap. The two edges of the floor can now be planed to a bevel, matching the angle of the end walls. Glue and pin the bannister wall and capping (cut from $\frac{1}{8}$in. scrap), and the upper dividing wall, in position. For added

strength glue a piece of $\frac{1}{4}$in. beading along the join of the upper wall and floor.

Chimney stack To make the chimney (see sketch), cut out a slot to the thickness of the side wall, but $\frac{1}{4}$in. shorter than its height. This $\frac{1}{4}$in. will allow you to glue a hearth, cut from scrap ply, to the base of the stack: before gluing this hearth in place, cut out the fireplace. The pot is made from scrap dowelling, drilled through the middle. For extra

strength in case of rough handling, screw through the side wall, as well as gluing the stack in position.

Balcony Again, construct from $\frac{1}{4}$in. ply; the amount of decoration is optional. The two end walls are glued and pinned to the front wall, and then the base is glued and pinned to these. Centre the balcony on the main beams and mark their positions on its underside. Now, drill two holes through the balcony floor, to take a $\frac{1}{2}$in. No. 6 screw, one

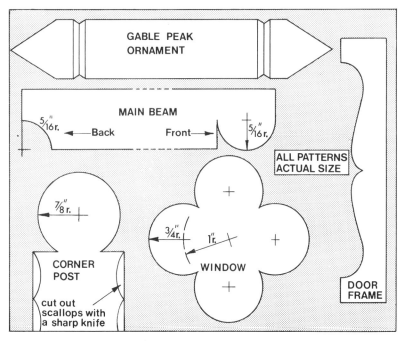

Labels within the figure:
GABLE PEAK ORNAMENT

MAIN BEAM

5/16 r. ←Back   Front→   5/16" r.

ALL PATTERNS ACTUAL SIZE

7/8 r.

3/4 r.   1" r.

CORNER POST

cut out scallops with a sharp knife

WINDOW

DOOR FRAME

screw to each beam. Pilot drill the beams to avoid them splitting. Finally, glue and screw the balcony in place, and add the capping (cut from $\frac{1}{8}$ in. scrap).

Door and window frames The window frames are $\frac{1}{2}$ in. wide, cut from $\frac{1}{8}$ in. timber. Cut the upright frames first. These should be a wedge-fit within the window aperture. The horizontal frames are next cut to wedge between the two uprights. Glue the frames in place, flush to the inside walls. The door frames are cut from $\frac{1}{4}$ in. square ramin beading, and they should slightly overlap the door aperture, so that the doors close snugly against them. The decorative elements are cut from $\frac{1}{8}$ in. scrap, and are optional (see pattern drawing).

Shutters Each shutter should be cut, using $\frac{1}{8}$ in. thick timber, to half the total width of the window. Drill the decorative holes, if required, and glue to the outside edges of the window frames.

Roof Mark out and cut the two main roof pieces from $\frac{1}{4}$ in. ply, allowing a fraction extra for safety at the ridge edge. Offer up each half, in

turn, to the house, and check the positions of the corner posts and chimney stack. If O.K., cut out the slots for these items, initially too short, gradually trimming down to an exact fit. Each side must be fitted individually until the final trimming of the ridge edges. When both halves are fitted to your satisfaction, plane the bevels along the ridge of each piece, to take the ridge capping. With these bevels completed, the two halves should sit comfortably over the whole house the two bevels coming together to form a flat ridge line.

Roof beams Mark off the four beams from 1 in. by $\frac{1}{4}$ in. timber, and cut slightly overlength: once again decorate before fitting. With the roof halves in place, offer up each beam, in turn, and mark the exact angle to cut at the ridge point. Check also that the roof beams, when fixed, will clear the corner posts, ensuring the easy removal of each half. Now, mark the position of each roof half slightly; this will ensure beam, and pre-pin the beams. The surest way of getting them to fit accurately, is to remove one roof half from the house, and then to

glue and pin the two roof beams to the remaining roof half. Having done this, remove the completed half, and repeat the procedure with the second half. Assemble both roof halves and check the vertical join of the beams, if this appears too tight, trim to an easy fit. Cut the two gable peak ornaments from scrap and glue to one half of the roof only. Finally, plane the ridge spar to a triangular section from $\frac{3}{4}$ in. by $\frac{3}{4}$ in. timber. It should be made to overlap each roof half slightly, this will ensure a neat finish when the tiles are glued on. Glue the spar along one roof half only, between the two peak ornaments. If, when assembled, the roof appears tight, gently ease down the bevel on the other ridge. The roof is now complete apart from the tiling. Cut the tiles from thin card, 2 in. by $1\frac{1}{2}$ in. by $\frac{1}{16}$ in. – you will need dozens. Start at one lower corner and stick them on, in rows, overlapping each succeeding row by about $\frac{1}{2}$ in. The vertical joins should also be staggered.

Finishing off The doll's house in the picture was given a white stucco treatment by the application of some old stone paint I had stored away in my garage. However, the same effect can be achieved by adding fine sand to any old tin of paint you may have, and giving it a good mix up. The colour of the mix is immaterial, as a coat of white emulsion, applied afterwards, gives the stucco a real professional look. The colours you pick for the general decoration of the house, are entirely up to you, but try to get the colours to compliment each other, or the final effect may well be spoiled. As yet I have not mentioned the fitting of the doors: these are best painted separately and fitted to the house when dry. Tiny, $\frac{1}{2}$ in. hinges are used, taking $\frac{1}{4}$ in. No. o screws (see chapter 2, page 22, for useful tip). Screw the hinges to the doors first, and then position the door towards the top of its frame, to avoid any slight drop, and screw it home.

Toy furniture

Although all the furniture illustrated has been specifically designed to match the house, the very simple methods of construction used can be adapted to suit any variety of architecture. There are no detailed joints to worry about, the units being easily assembled using adhesive and occasionally light pinning (see sketches). Most of these units are made from scrap timber but certain stock-sized materials will, nevertheless, be useful to you: strip mouldings of varying sections and widths; $\frac{1}{4}$in. and $\frac{1}{8}$in. sheet, either ply or solid timber and easily cut with a sharp knife; dowel rods of all sizes, for the legs of tables and chairs; and finally wooden balls and beads. Always be on the look-out for extra items which, with a little imagination, could easily be adapted as furnishings.

Soft furnishings, such as bedcovers and easy chairs, can sometimes prove a bit tricky to reproduce. To overcome this problem, shape the unit to a basic form and then, using a contact adhesive, stick the cloth covering in place.

Aside from all the basic units, i.e. a bed for the bedroom, a cooker for the kitchen, give the house added interest by including the little extras that we all collect in our homes. Pictures on the wall can be made from miniatures, cut from magazines and mounted on card or thin ply; a yard broom needs only a few odd bristles, or dried grass, bound to the end of a piece of dowel; a wooden bead adapts simply into a flower vase, etc.

Finally, if you want to introduce some residents for the house, adapt the ideas found elsewhere in the book and, bearing in mind the relevant scale, make up some suitable figures.

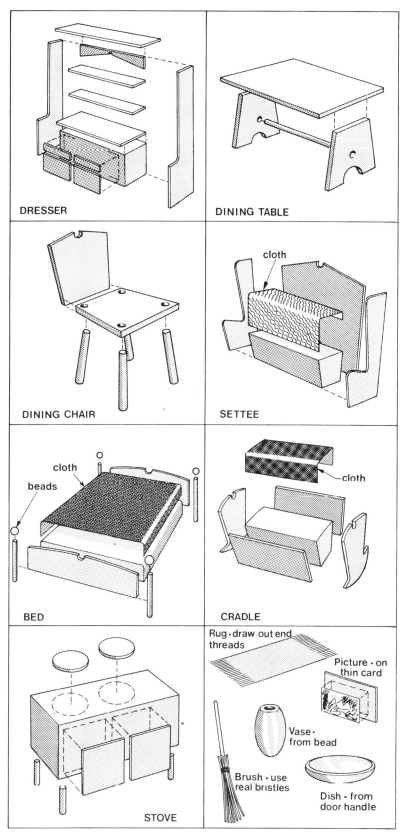

DRESSER

DINING TABLE

DINING CHAIR

cloth

SETTEE

cloth
beads

BED

cloth

CRADLE

STOVE

Rug · draw out end threads

Picture · on thin card

Vase · from bead

Brush · use real bristles

Dish · from door handle

Fairground Roundabout

Illustrated in colour on page 26

Materials

$1\frac{1}{4}'' \times \frac{5}{8}'' \times 3'$ pine (support base)
$5'' \times \frac{1}{2}'' \times 2'$ pine (pulley wheels, cage assembly)
$\frac{5}{8}''$ dia. $\times 2''$ dowel (washers)
$\frac{1}{4}''$ dia. $\times 8'$ dowel (cage supports, boat arms)
$\frac{3}{16}''$ dia. $\times 1'$ dowel (head pegs)
$1''$ dia. wooden balls (10) (figures, etc.)
$1\frac{1}{2}''$ No. 6 flathead screw (1)
fine string, adhesive

CONSTRUCTION

Base unit Mark off and cut to length, from $1\frac{1}{4}$in. by $\frac{5}{8}$in. timber, the two main cross beams. Clamp them together and, using a coping saw, cut out the fancy ends; this will ensure that the ends are matched. The two beams are held together by a simple half-housing joint (see page 20) and this can now be cut. Remember, too tight a fit is better than a sloppy one. Having done this, sand thoroughly and glue the two cross beams together, checking with your try square that they meet at right angles. Mark on the centres for the two pulley axles.

Pulley assembly Cut two discs, 4in. diameter, from $\frac{1}{2}$in. thick timber – again using your coping saw. Clean them up with a flat file and sand thoroughly. Take each disc in turn and, using soft packing pieces, clamp it firmly in the vice. Now, with a $\frac{1}{4}$in. round file, cut a groove all the way round the edge of the disc, moving it within the vice as your cut progresses: the groove need not be any deeper than $\frac{1}{8}$in. This completes the two pulley wheels. The outer, or drive, wheel should now be drilled for the axle and turning handle, both of which are cut from $\frac{1}{4}$in. dowel rod. Drill half-way through for the handle and glue in position. Cut the axle, overlong at this stage, and having drilled the base unit, glue it in place. The inner pulley wheel is

centred on a screw axle ($1\frac{1}{2}$in. No. 6 screw); drill and countersink the axle hole, and pilot drill the cross beams. Cut three washers from $\frac{5}{8}$in. dowel rod, about $\frac{3}{16}$in. thick. Two of these are for the drive wheel and one for the inner wheel; drill their centres accordingly. They should have an easy fit on the two axles. Assemble the pulley wheels on the base unit and fit a string drive-belt (a long elastic band is even better). Check that the assembly operates smoothly and is not too sloppy. The drive-wheel axle can now be cut to length and topped off with a 1in. diameter wooden ball. A spot of candle-grease on the axles will improve the smoothness of their operation.

Roundabout barrel Cut two discs, 5in. diameter, from $\frac{1}{2}$in. thick timber. Clean them up thoroughly but don't lose their centre points. Clamp them together and mark out and drill the eight holes for the upright supports. These are all made from $\frac{1}{4}$in. dowel rod. Remove the inner pulley from the base unit and clamp it to one of the barrel discs with their centres aligning. Mark on the pulley wheel the positions of the four location pegs and drill right through both discs. The location pegs are also made from $\frac{1}{4}$in. dowel rod and can now be cut and glued in the pulley wheel. Cut them long enough to protrude right through the lower

disc of the roundabout barrel when assembled. The location holes in the barrel disc should be opened out to allow an easy push fit over the pegs. If they are too tight, ease them with a piece of sandpaper wrapped around a dowel rod. To make sure that the four pegs will always find their respective holes in the barrel disc, partially assemble the discs together while the glue holding the pegs in place is still setting. Once set, trim off any excess dowel from below the inner pulley wheel and re-fit to the base unit. Now, mark on the edge of the upper barrel disc the positions of the eight swing-boat spokes. Carry these marking lines right across the top of the disc, through the centre point. The spokes are also made from $\frac{1}{4}$in. dowel rod, so drill the holes for these to a depth of $\frac{3}{4}$in. Take care that the angle of the drill is always pointing to the exact centre of the disc, aligning the drill along the marking line. Now cut the eight support poles from $\frac{1}{4}$in. dowel rod. These should be cut overlong at this stage. Round off one end only of each pole. This will be the top end and will protrude through the top disc by $\frac{1}{4}$in. Glue the poles into the top disc setting them through to the right distance. When the assembly is dry, turn the top disc on to its back and push the bottom disc on to the poles. To ensure that this is the same distance from the top

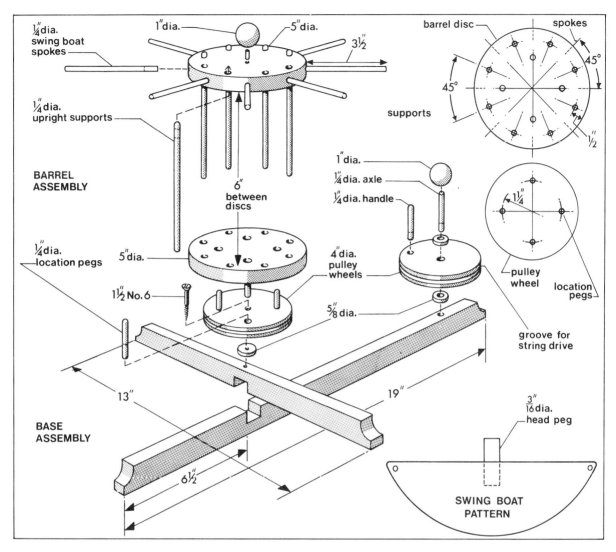

$\frac{1}{4}''$ dia. swing boat spokes

$1''$ dia.

$5''$ dia.

$3\frac{1}{2}$

barrel disc

spokes

$45°$

$45°$

supports

$\frac{1}{2}''$

$\frac{1}{4}''$ dia. upright supports

BARREL ASSEMBLY

$6''$ between discs

$1''$ dia.

$\frac{1}{4}''$ dia. axle

$\frac{1}{4}''$ dia. handle

$1\frac{1}{4}''$

$\frac{1}{4}''$ dia. location pegs

$5''$ dia.

$4''$ dia. pulley wheels

pulley wheel

location pegs

$1\frac{1}{2}$ No. 6

$5\frac{5}{8}''$ dia.

groove for string drive

$13''$

$19''$

$\frac{3}{16}''$ dia. head peg

BASE ASSEMBLY

$6\frac{1}{2}''$

SWING BOAT PATTERN

disc all the way round, cut a piece of scrap to the required length and insert this alongside each pole in turn, pushing the bottom disc down to this mark as you go round. Any excess dowel poking through the bottom can now be trimmed off. Mark off and cut the eight swing-boat spokes from $\frac{1}{4}$in. dowel; again cut them overlong at this stage. Glue them into the top disc, aligning them to the centre. If a spoke does not appear to run true to the centre, open out the hole slightly and re-align. Each spoke should be $3\frac{1}{2}$in. long, measured from the edge of the disc, so mark off and trim to length. Finish by nicely rounding off the end of each spoke. All that

now remains to complete the roundabout barrel is to cap off the top disc with a 1in. wooden ball.

Swing boats Trace off the shape of the swing boats from the pattern drawing, and transfer on to $\frac{1}{2}$in. thick timber – eight times. Cut out the boats and sand thoroughly. Take each boat and drill a small hole through each end for the support strings and a $\frac{3}{16}$in. hole in the centre for the figure mounting. The figures are made from 1in. diameter wooden balls. These should now be drilled, as indicated, for mounting on each boat. If the figures are to be painted then it is best done *before* they are fixed to the boats.

Finishing off Apply a good wax polish to the whole structure. Mount each of the figures with a little adhesive on its boat and thread through the support strings. Each boat can either be tied to its respective spoke or the end of the spoke can be drilled and the string threaded through, the latter arrangement being the neater of the two.

Assemble the whole roundabout and adjust the height of the swing boats to avoid any fouling of the mechanism. When you have made the necessary adjustments apply a touch of adhesive to each spoke to prevent the support strings from slipping.

Trolley

Illustrated in colour on page 54

Materials

$9'' \times \frac{5}{8}'' \times 4'$ parana pine (structure)
$1\frac{1}{4}''$ No. 6 raised-head screws (12)
    No. 6 screw cups (12)
 $1''$ No. 6 flathead screws (2)
$1\frac{1}{4}''$ No. 6 flathead screws (4)
Fobel plastic wheel kit, $3''$ dia.
$\frac{1}{4}''$ dia. $\times 2''$ steel bolt
adhesive

This toy was designed primarily as a brick cart, for the younger child. Its interior dimensions permit the transportation of 20, large-size, wooden bricks. It can be made with an enclosed box carrier or it can be left with an open front, as illustrated. It has been fitted with a Fobel wheel system, using 3in. wheels, and the simple steering mechanism allows easy movement and allays some of the frustrations felt with less easily manipulated trucks. In its open-fronted form, by doubling all the stated dimensions except the timber thickness,★ it converts into a speedy go-cart for the older child.

CONSTRUCTION

Trolley assembly Mark out and cut to size, from $\frac{5}{8}$in. thick timber, the four main body pieces: the base, the two sides and the back. Include the positions of all the holes to be drilled. If you intend to have a closed-box carrier, then also mark out and cut the front cross piece. Clean up all the parts thoroughly to a smooth finish. The front axle pivot-spindle is a $\frac{1}{4}$in. steel bolt, so drill the hole at the front of the base to accommodate the spindle. Next, cut the rear axle support brace to length, and pilot drill the screw holes. These should take a No. 6 screw; countersink both the holes. Using 1in. No. 6 screws, glue and screw the rear axle brace to the base. Pilot drill the fixing holes in

the back, again for No. 6 screws, but do not countersink them this time. All the exterior screw fixings are $1\frac{1}{4}$in. No. 6 raised-head screws, each used with a screw cup: now glue and screw the back piece to the base. If you do not want an open-fronted truck, the front cross piece will now have to be fitted. Pilot drill through the base, countersinking both the holes on the underside. Now, using $1\frac{1}{4}$in. No. 6 screws, glue the front piece in position and screw up through the base. Offer up each side, in turn, and check the position of the axle hole. Drill this hole to accommodate the steel axle (it can afford to be a tight fit, as the wheels are a loose fit over the axle), and pilot drill the holes for the exterior screw fixings. Glue and screw one side to the base assembly. Slide in the axle and check that the second side piece is square, and aligning, before finally gluing and screwing it in position. The main trolley assembly is now complete.

Front axle Mark out and cut the axle spar and the two internal mudguards; these act as an anchorage for the two axle ends. Clean up the parts thoroughly and drill the spar for the pivot-spindle bolt and the towing string. Note that the pivot hole is not quite on the centre line but a little behind the axle. Offer up each mudguard in turn against the axle spar and check the

positions of the axle holes; drill these and the two pilot holes for the screw fixings in each mudguard. Countersink the pilot holes on the outside face. Using $1\frac{1}{4}$in. No. 6 screws, glue and screw the mudguards to the front spar; once again check the axle alignment before finally fixing the second mudguard. The two trolley sections are now completed and, if required, should be painted or varnished before fitting the wheel assemblies in position.

Wheel assembly Tap one hub-cap on to one end of each axle only. Slide the two axles, complete with their wheels, into the two trolley sections and mark off the correct length; remove the axles and cut to length. Re-assemble and tap on the outer hub-caps. Finally, insert the $\frac{1}{4}$in. pivot bolt and screw up. There should be a washer against each wood face, including between the axle and the base, to ensure smooth operation. To avoid the nut unscrewing itself from the bolt, drill a small hole through the bolt immediately below the tightened nut and insert a split pin. Alternatively, use two nuts tightened up really hard against each other.

★To make the go-cart for the older child the timber thickness need only be increased to 1in., and the pivot bolt to $\frac{5}{16}$in. diameter.

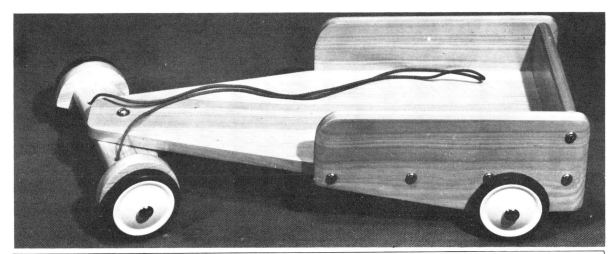

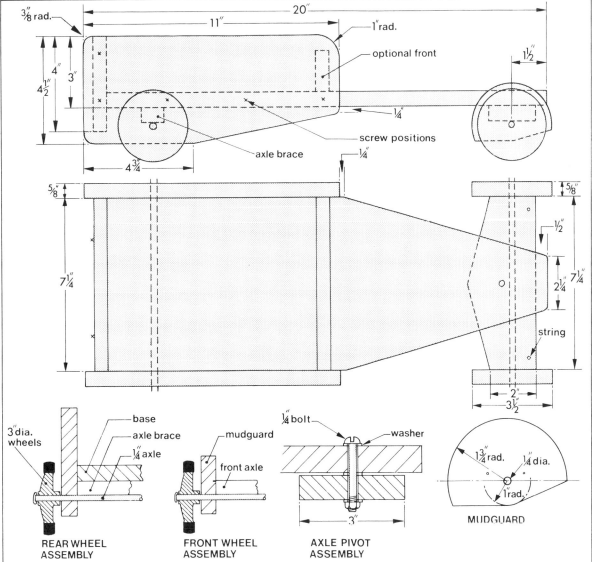

$\frac{3}{8}''$ rad.

20"

11"

1" rad.

optional front

1$\frac{1}{2}''$

4"

3"

4$\frac{1}{2}''$

$\frac{1}{4}''$

screw positions

axle brace

4$\frac{3}{4}$

$\frac{1}{4}''$

$\frac{5}{8}''$

$\frac{5}{8}''$

$\frac{1}{2}''$

7$\frac{1}{4}''$

7$\frac{1}{4}$

2$\frac{1}{4}''$

string

2"

3$\frac{1}{2}$

base

3" dia.
wheels

axle brace

$\frac{1}{4}''$ axle

mudguard

front axle

$\frac{1}{4}''$ bolt

washer

1$\frac{3}{4}''$ rad.

$\frac{1}{4}''$ dia.

$\frac{1}{2}''$ rad.

3"

MUDGUARD

REAR WHEEL
ASSEMBLY

FRONT WHEEL
ASSEMBLY

AXLE PIVOT
ASSEMBLY

Simple Figures

Illustrated in colour on page 23

Materials
wooden balls, all sizes
dowel rod, all sizes
scrap timber
adhesive, etc.

The making of these characters, and their animal friends is extremely simple. Each one can be made in a very short space of time, with the minimum of materials, and consequently expense. The materials needed are listed, rather vaguely, above, and you will find when you come to make your own figures, why I have been so vague. Their creation emphasizes, yet again, the importance of being a hoarder, and never throwing away any scrap of timber, no matter how small. For instance, the hippopotamus was created from the two remaining halves of the wooden balls, used to make the lights on the fire engine (see page 56); with the addition of the second, slightly larger, ball, I found I had all the materials needed to complete him. The caterpillar was made from the left over, badly drilled, beads (none of us is perfect), used on the abacus (see page 38); the holes being off-centre, they lent themselves splendidly to the twisting shape of a caterpillar; his antenae are bristles from a kitchen broom. The tortoise, also uses a spare bead from the abacus for his head: so does the penguin, which has a body made from scrap pine, and wings and feet cut from thin ply. The hedgehog is the other half of the tortoise, again using bristles (taken from my now, virtually bald, broom). The little brown monkey swings from a converted coat hanger, with the ends well bedded in a solid piece of scrap. The pig speaks for itself. The Chinaman has feet made from scrap pine and a cupboard door handle hat, his arms swinging on small brass upholstery pins; the body and head have been left unglued to spin freely around the centre dowel. There are many other creatures and characters, within the imagination, that can be created from these simple shapes and scraps; each one of them having his own individual personality, bestowed by the expression painted on his face. They can be painted in gay colours, their slightly whimsical nature precluding the use of realistic colouring.

NOTE: For drilling some of the tiny holes on the figures, it would be useful, but not essential, to purchase a pin-chuck drill. These are operated like a pencil and twisted between the fingers. They are also relatively inexpensive.

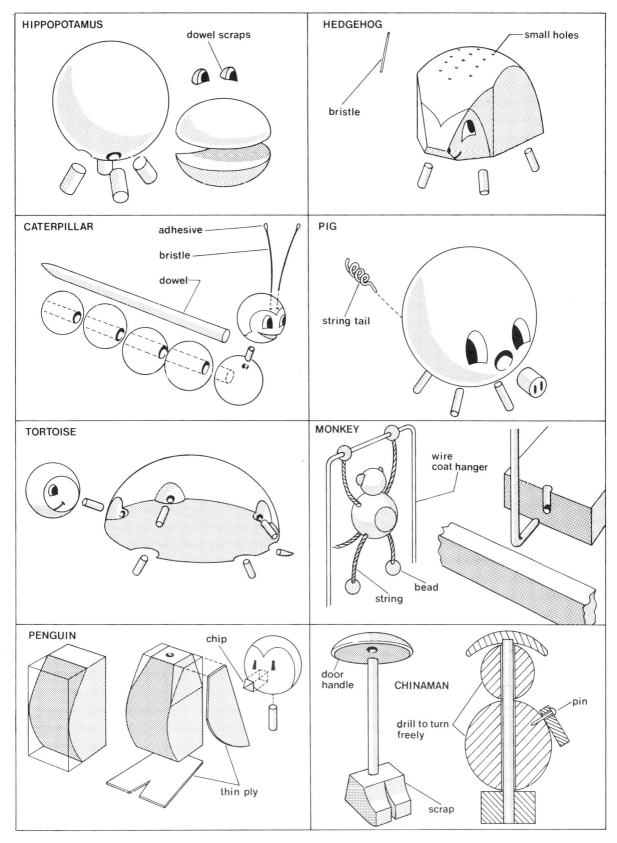

HIPPOPOTAMUS

dowel scraps

HEDGEHOG

small holes

bristle

CATERPILLAR

adhesive

bristle

dowel

PIG

string tail

TORTOISE

MONKEY

wire coat hanger

bead

string

PENGUIN

chip

thin ply

door handle

CHINAMAN

drill to turn freely

pin

scrap

73

Toybox

Illustrated in colour on page 30

Materials

6′ × 3′ hardboard sheet
2″ × 1″ × 10″ (3 pieces)
1″ × 1″ × 10″ (3 pieces)
$\frac{1}{4}$″ × 5′ quadrant
1$\frac{1}{2}$″ No. 6 raised-head screws and cups (24)
1$\frac{1}{4}$″ No. 6 flathead screws (24)
$\frac{3}{4}$″ No. 6 flathead screws (24)
$\frac{1}{2}$″ No. 6 flathead screws (12)
$\frac{1}{2}$″ panel pins
2$\frac{1}{2}$″ hinges (2), as illustrated

CONSTRUCTION

Inner frame assembly Both the top frame and the base frame are cut from 1in. by 1in. timber. Each one measures 34in. by 14in. Cut all the lengths required and cut the half-lap joints at each corner and the centre strut on the base frame; also cut out the housings for the hinge support braces.

At a later stage the inner base frame will be screwed to the outer base frame, from the inside, so pilot drill two or three holes for a No. 6 screw along each rail, countersinking on the inside. Using $\frac{3}{4}$in. No. 6 screws assemble both frames. From 2in. by 1in. timber cut the hinge brace struts, 14in. long; half-lap each end and with the two frames held vertically and square to each other, fit the two braces, thus locking the frames together.

Panels All the panels are $\frac{1}{8}$in. thick hardboard sheet. Cut out the floor panel, 14in. by 34in., and the two notches for the hinge braces, pin in place. Now cut the two end panels, 14in. wide and 13$\frac{5}{8}$in. high (see section A), and pin to each end of the frame assembly flush to the base. Finally, cut the side panels to the same height, but allow for the extra thickness of the two ends; 13$\frac{5}{8}$in. by 34$\frac{1}{4}$in. Pin the side panels in place.★

Outer frame assembly Both the centre frame and base frame are cut from 2in. by 1in. timber. Start by cutting the end rails to the total width of the box, 14$\frac{1}{4}$in. Turn the box upside-down, and using 1$\frac{1}{4}$in. No. 6 screws, fit the base rails in place, screwing through the pre-drilled holes in the inner frame. Now fit the centre end rails, screwing through the hardboard panel with $\frac{1}{2}$in. No. 6 screws. The long side rails, which overlap the ends, can now be cut; check the exact length of the box before cutting. Drill two holes in the end of each rail to take a No. 6 screw but do not countersink these holes. Fit the rails, as previously, and finish by screwing tight each of the corner butt joints with 1$\frac{1}{2}$in. No. 6 raised-head screws and cups. Finally, seal each of the vertical hardboard joins with a strip of $\frac{1}{4}$in. quadrant glued in place.

Lid Make up the inner frame from 1in. by 1in. timber, exactly as for the inner base frame of the box – including the pilot holes. All the dimensions are identical, 14in. by 34in. Cut the top panel to the exact size of the inner frame.

The outer frame is cut from 2in. by 1in. timber. Cut the end rails to 14in., this being the total width of the box, and fit to the inner frame

(see drawing for exact position). With both end rails fitted, check the exact length of the lid and cut the side rails: drill the ends for the screw fixings and fit in place on the lid assembly. Finally, drop in the top panel and pin all round.

Hinges Place the lid over the box and mark off the two positions for the hinges, aligning them exactly with the two hinge brace struts. Remove the lid and screw the hinges to the underside of the rear rail; they will not require slots and can be surface fitted. Before finally screwing the lid on to the box, insert some scraps of thin card, about $\frac{1}{16}$in. thick, between the rear rail of the box and the rear rail of the lid (see sketch), this will ensure the lid fitting snugly over the front rail of the box.

★If you intend to paint the toybox, now is a good time to do it, without the hamper of all the outer rails. The broad, brightly coloured stripes are very effective, but the choice of decoration is yours. The outer rails can also be varnished, you will need at least three coats for a good hard-wearing finish, before they are fitted to the box assembly.

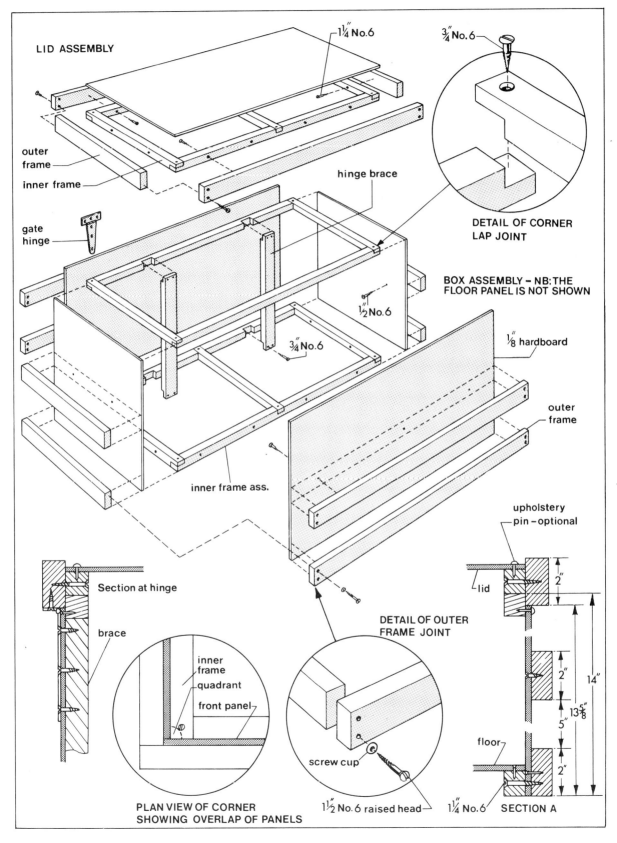

LID ASSEMBLY

$1\frac{1}{4}''$ No.6

$\frac{3}{4}''$ No.6

outer frame

inner frame

gate hinge

hinge brace

DETAIL OF CORNER LAP JOINT

BOX ASSEMBLY – NB: THE FLOOR PANEL IS NOT SHOWN

$\frac{1}{2}''$ No.6

$\frac{3}{4}''$ No.6

$\frac{1}{8}''$ hardboard

outer frame

inner frame ass.

Section at hinge

brace

inner frame

quadrant

front panel

upholstery pin – optional

lid

2"

2"

14"

$13\frac{5}{8}''$

5"

floor

2"

PLAN VIEW OF CORNER SHOWING OVERLAP OF PANELS

screw cup

$1\frac{1}{2}''$ No.6 raised head

$1\frac{1}{4}''$ No.6

DETAIL OF OUTER FRAME JOINT

SECTION A

Glossary of terms

BEVEL
The edge of a board, or block, cut at an angle

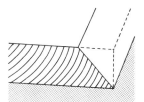

BOND
A glued joint

BUTT JOINT
One of the simplest joints used to join two pieces of timber together

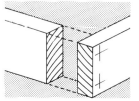

CHAMFER
The corner of a board, or block, cut at an angle

COUNTERSINK
The recess bored to receive the head of a flathead screw, making it flush with the timber surface

DATUM LINE
A true, accurate line from which all other dimensions can be measured or plotted

DOWEL ROD
A hardwood moulding, machined to a round section

ENCLOSED CUT
An area of waste within a component part, totally surrounded by the required timber of that part

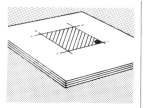

FIGURING
The decorative result of the combined colouring and grain pattern of timber

GRAIN
The natural direction of the timber fibres

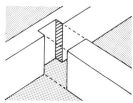

HOUSING
A section cut away from a piece of timber to locate or accommodate an adjoining component

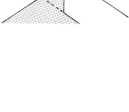

LAYING OFF
When painting: the final strokes made softly before lifting the brush from the surface

MOULDING
Strips of hardwood timber machined in a variety of sections

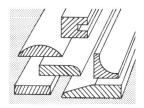

OFFER UP, TO
To test fit a component part on an assembly prior to its final fixing

PACKING PIECE
Softwood scraps used within a bench vice to protect the workpiece surface whilst clamped

PRE-PINNING
The insertion of panel pins in a free component prior to it being finally fixed to an assembly

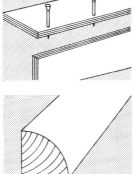

QUADRANT
A moulding, one quarter of a complete circle in section, the size qualified by the width of the flat face

ROSE BIT
A special-purpose drill bit designed for cutting countersink recesses

TOPCOAT
The final application of a paint or varnish

WASTE
The area of timber to be cut away from a marked off component

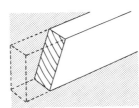

WORKPIECE
The timber component being currently worked

Metric equivalents

Although it is still possible to purchase timber in Imperial sizes, since 1970 more and more suppliers have been cutting their timber to Metric stock sizes. In all probability you will be offered these stocks when you make a purchase. For that reason you may find the following tables of use.

Conversion, inches to millimetres

in.	mm.	in.	mm.	in.	mm.
$\frac{1}{16}$	1.59	$1\frac{1}{8}$	28.57	$3\frac{1}{4}$	82.55
$\frac{1}{8}$	3.17	$1\frac{1}{4}$	31.35	$3\frac{1}{2}$	88.90
$\frac{3}{16}$	4.76	$1\frac{3}{8}$	34.92	$3\frac{3}{4}$	95.25
$\frac{1}{4}$	6.35	$1\frac{1}{2}$	38.10	4	101.60
$\frac{5}{16}$	7.94	$1\frac{5}{8}$	41.27	5	127.00
$\frac{3}{8}$	9.52	$1\frac{3}{4}$	44.45	6	152.40
$\frac{7}{16}$	11.11	$1\frac{7}{8}$	47.62	7	177.80
$\frac{1}{2}$	12.70	2	50.80	8	203.20
$\frac{5}{8}$	15.87	$2\frac{1}{4}$	57.15	9	228.60
$\frac{3}{4}$	19.05	$2\frac{1}{2}$	63.50	10	254.00
$\frac{7}{8}$	22.22	$2\frac{3}{4}$	69.85	11	279.40
1	25.40	3	76.20	12	304.80

Conversion, feet to metres

ft.	m.	ft.	m.	ft.	m.
1	0.304	5	1.520	9	2.740
2	0.608	6	1.820	10	3.050
3	0.912	7	2.130	11	3.350
4	1.210	8	2.430	12	3.660

Metric sizes in sawn timber
thickness × width (millimetres)

	75	100	125	150	175	200	225	250	300
16	★	★	★	★					
19	★	★	★	★					
22	★	★	★	★					
25	★	★	★	★	★	★	★	★	★
32	★	★	★	★	★	★	★	★	★
38	★	★	★	★	★	★	★		
44	★	★	★	★	★	★	★	★	★
50	★	★	★	★	★	★	★	★	★
63		★	★	★	★	★	★		
75		★	★	★	★	★	★	★	★
100		★		★		★		★	★
150			★			★			★

Index

Acknowledgements

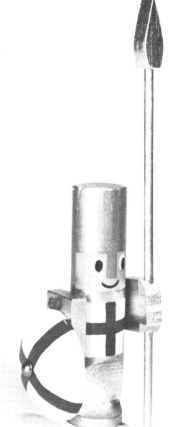

I would like to thank the following people for their help and advice in the preparation of this book.

My special thanks go to Mr. John F. Adams and his wife of 'Woodcraft', Crowborough Hill, Crowborough, Sussex. Their shop was the main source of the materials and equipment used in the construction of the projects featured, and their helpful service has been very much appreciated. Mr. Adams also kindly loaned the tools for the photograph on page 6.

Mr. Kevin Grimmer of Alpha Plus Studios, Leatherhead, for taking so much trouble over the photographs.

And last, but by no means least, my wife, who not only typed out the manuscript but tolerated a disrupted household for the period it took to complete the toys.